TABLE C

Rug Hooking Presents

B·A·S·I·C
RUG HOOKING

With "A Beginner's Guide"
by Verna P. Cox

Editor
Wyatt R. Myers

Book Designer
Cher Williams

Assistant Editor
Lisa McMullen

Photography
Impact Xpozures

Chairman
M. David Detweiler

Publisher
J. Richard Noel

Presented by

R·U·G
HOOKING

1300 Market St., Suite 202
Lemoyne, PA 17043-1420

(717) 234-5091

(800) 233-9055

www.rughookingonline.com

PRINTED IN CHINA

As I began planning book projects for 2003, I noticed a very interesting trend in the books *Rug Hooking* has done of late: While we have covered a delightful range of interesting topics, very few books have been focused on beginners. In fact, the last beginner's book we published was *Basic Rug Hooking*, way back in 1990!

Thinking about this, I realized it was time for a change. Especially when you consider all the wonderful beginner's material we present in *Rug Hooking* magazine.

Keeping this in mind, we are very proud to present a new *Basic Rug Hooking*, just in time to start a summer craft project! And this *Basic Rug Hooking* has tons of useful information. An all-new introduction for beginners and 12 of *Rug Hooking* magazine's all-time best beginner projects are packed inside this little book.

> "Regardless of how you want to get started in the craft of rug hooking, I guarantee that this book has a project for you."
> —Wyatt Myers

Regardless of how you want to get started in the craft of rug hooking, I guarantee that this book has a project for you. Are holiday crafts your cup of tea? See the *Christmas Stocking* on page 31 or *Pumpkin Moonshine* on page 52. How about a *Patriotic Heart* to show your pride in America? It's on page 43. And whether you want to create a realistic looking rug, one with a more primitive style, or even a classic Oriental design, *Basic Rug Hooking* has the pattern for you. Plus, this book includes a pull-out pattern with four exclusive designs!

As a beginner myself, I can personally attest that *Basic Rug Hooking* has everything you need to begin hooking rugs. If you're a beginner, welcome to the fold. And if you're a teacher, be sure to share all the projects in *Basic Rug Hooking* with somebody new. Open a whole new world to them with wool!

Wyatt Myers

ABOUT THE PUBLISHER

Rug Hooking magazine, the publisher of *Basic Rug Hooking*, welcomes you to the rug hooking community. Since 1989 *Rug Hooking* has served thousands of rug hookers around the world with its instructional, illustrated articles on dyeing, designing, color planning, hooking techniques, and more. Each issue of the magazine contains color photographs of beautiful rugs old and new, profiles of teachers, designers, and fellow rug hookers, and announcements of workshops, exhibits, and gatherings.

Rug Hooking has responded to its readers' demand for more inspiration and information by establishing an inviting, informative website at *www.rughookingonline.com* and by publishing a number of books on this fiber art. Along with how-to pattern books and a Sourcebook listing of teachers, guilds, and schools, *Rug Hooking* has produced the competition-based book series *A Celebration of Hand-Hooked Rugs*, now in its 13th year.

The hand-hooked rugs you'll see in *Basic Rug Hooking* represent just a fragment of the incredible art that is being produced today by women and men of all ages. For more information on rug hooking and *Rug Hooking* magazine, call or write us at the address on page 1.

by Verna P. Cox

HISTORY

Primitive rug hooking was a craft born in the early 1800s. At that time, burlap was introduced to the farmer's wife in the form of "feed bags." Once the bags were empty, the burlap was washed and stretched over frames to be used for rug hooking projects. Plain pictures of farm and home life appeared on the burlap, and old clothing scraps were cut up in narrow strips for the hooking. Usually, the art objects in the pictures were outlined with dark colors, and the brighter and lighter colors were used to hook in between the lines.

Even though yarn and other fibers were used in this type of rug hooking, the lightweight woolen fabric found in men and women's clothing was by far the most popular. The plaid fabrics were wonderful to use, and when more colors were needed, some of the fabric was dyed with natural home dyes. Most of the strips used for hooking then were about $1/4$" wide and were hooked using a medium hook. Sometimes the backgrounds were hooked with a wider $1/2$" strip. When details were needed, narrower $1/8$" strips were used.

In later years, primitive rug hooking techniques changed. Color dyeing became very specific. New color dyes were available at local stores, and women's clubs started having classes. Even though the process of pulling up loops through the burlap was the same, the art in traditional rug hooking became more detailed and more realistic. The strips became narrower, from $1/16$" to $1/8$", and a finer hook was used. A new invention called the "hooking cutter" was introduced, allowing the creation of more than one strip at a time.

Today, these two views of rug hooking are still widely practiced. Hooking with wide strips ($1/4$" to $1/2$") is known as primitive rug hooking. Hooking with fine strips ($1/16$" to $1/8$") is known as traditional rug hooking.

ABOUT THE AUTHOR

Verna Cox, a Maine native, has been traditional rug braiding for 45 years. When she was young, she was exposed to many crafts, but braiding captured most of her time and energy. She has appeared in the pages of *Woman's Day*, *Family Circle*, *Rug Hooking* magazine, *Down East* magazine, *Country Woman*, various decorating magazines, and has been featured in news stories and talk shows on both commercial TV and PBS.

Verna has developed an illustrated instructional manual about traditional rug braiding and five braiding and hooking videos. Her instructional booklet for beginning rug hookers is included in its entirety here.

MATERIALS NEEDED

BACKING FABRIC

Any open weave fabric can be used, as long as it will allow you to pull hooking strips up through the fabric. The most popular backing fabrics are burlap, monk's cloth, and linen. You will find various weights and styles of these fabrics. Hooking companies have many different types of backing fabrics available, depending on whether you want to do fine hooking or primitive hooking. The crucial difference in these two styles of hooking is the width of strips being used. You need to select the proper backing to accommodate the size of hooking strip you have decided to use.

HOOKING STRIPS

The fabric you plan to use for the actual rug hooking is your choice. In the old primitive rugs, everything was used from yarn to cotton, as well as wool. In traditional hooking, fine, lightweight wool from men's suits was used, and the strips were cut $1/16$" to $1/8$" in width. This same lightweight wool was also used for primitive rugs, only the strips were cut wider ($1/4$" to $1/2$"). If you want to use cotton for hooking, you may want to cut (or tear) the strands at least $1/2$" wide. Denim can also be used, but you may want to cut the fabric about $1/8$" because it is such a firm fabric.

Knowing the amount of fabric needed for a project is an important consideration to make before beginning. The usual measurement is four times the area covered. For instance, a 4" square section is 4" x 4" sq. = 16, so the 4" square will require a 16 sq. inch section of hooking cloth.

FRAME

A frame is used to keep the backing fabric relatively stiff. Your frame of choice can be as inexpensive as an old picture frame or as expensive as a new hooking frame. If you are using soft material like monk's cloth or linen, you can use a regular embroidery hoop, but if you need something larger, you can use an old picture frame so that you can staple or tack the backing fabric to it. I found that canvas stretchers, sold in art stores, work well and are sold in many sizes. When working on large rugs, quilting frames are also used sometimes.

SOURCES: *For a list of companies that offer all the material needed for rug hooking, see the "Sources" section on page 63.*

HOOKS

Typically, rug hooks are shaped like a crochet hook and come in three sizes: small, medium, and large. They have a wooden handle to help you hold on to the hook more easily. I have found that the medium hook seems to be a good size for a beginner.

HOOKING CUTTERS

You do not actually need a hooking cutter, as you can cut your strips by hand. If you are working on a large project and feel you need the help, however, a cutter is wonderful. Cutters come with various sizes of blades, so you can cut fabric to your desired width. Usually you order one size of blade with the cutter and order other blades as you need them to cut wider or narrower widths. The $1/8$" blade cutter cuts four strands at a time, whereas the wider blades cut fewer strands. The cutter and blades are very durable and can be used for years and years without repair.

DESIGN

A multitude of different patterns are available on the market. Catalogs are available for you to select your pattern of choice. (You also have 12 lovely designs to choose from in this book!) In some cases you can order a design as part of a kit in which all the fabric has been pre-cut for you. A color photograph is usually a part of this kit as well, so you can understand where colors go. You can also design your own project if you wish. Use your own art design or copy a drawing from a coloring book. Using a permanent marker, draw the design that you desire onto backing fabric.

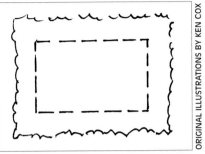

ORIGINAL ILLUSTRATIONS BY KEN COX

1 Cut out the backing fabric at least 3" to 4" larger (all around) than what the design will require. Remember that at times you will need extra fabric to attach to the frame. With a backing fabric that has a tendency to fray or unravel, use tape or sew the edges so that they will not unravel.

2 If you are doing your own design, tape the backing fabric to a firm surface (table, cardboard, etc.), so the fabric remains stiff and straight while you draw on the design. If drawing your own design, simply use a permanent marker.

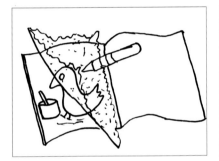

3 If you are copying an existing design, you can use a tracing fabric called Red Dot available at craft shops. Notice that a marker is used to trace the artwork from the book, then to the backing fabric.

FRAMES

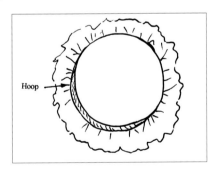

Hoop

1 If you are using soft backing fabric, such as monk's cloth or linen, then an embroidery hoop can work well depending upon the size of your design. A stiffer fabric, such as burlap, is usually too tough for a hoop.

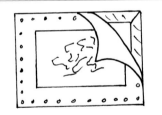

2 If you are not using a hoop, then you can use an old picture frame or canvas-stretcher found in most department stores and art supply stores. Using thumbtacks or a staple gun, simply attach the backing fabric to the frame, ready for rug hooking. If your design is larger than the frame will allow, then start your work on one side of the design. When you're finished with that section, remove it from the frame and move the frame over to the unfinished side of the design.

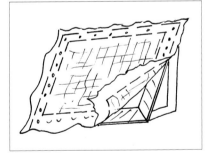

3 If your backing fabric is not large enough to reach the frame properly, simply sew a strip of strong fabric around the outer edge of the backing fabric. This sewing can be done by machine very easily or by hand if you wish. (There are many choices in frames. See the "Sources" section on page 63.)

FINDING FABRIC

METHOD 1

The easy choice would be to purchase wool in yardage for your project. The amount of fabric needed is four times the size of the section to be hooked in that color.

METHOD 2

The next choice is to collect old garments. Oftentimes, old plaids or tweeds provide just the colors you need. Yard sales and flea markets are good spots for finding old clothes. The garments need to be taken apart and washed with soap—hot wash, cold rinse—and dried with a dryer. This will shrink the fabric to make it easier to hook and more durable.

METHOD 3

With primitive rug hooking, bold colors work very well, but with traditional rug hooking, the artwork is generally hooked with more detail and more shading. This technique is sometimes achieved by purchasing the shades already color-dyed by companies, but you can also create your own colors and shades of colors by color-dyeing fabric in your own kitchen.

COLOR DYEING

a. Pre-wash fabric, or pre-soak in warm, sudsy water using dishwashing liquid or a wetting agent such as Synthrapol or Wetter Than Wet.

b. Use a large enamel pan on top of your stove. Cover counters to protect from dyes. All equipment, such as long forks, tongs, cleaning sponges, rubber gloves and pans, are to be kept just for dyeing. The color dye is diluted into a liquid form and can be kept in jars for long periods of time. The large enamel pan is called the "dye bath," and it holds boiling water, vinegar (to set the color), and the proper amount of dye needed for the size fabric you are working with. (It is smart to do a small test piece first). There are many ways of color dyeing—please realize that this is only one way.

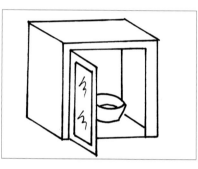

* Microwave ovens can also be used in the dyeing of fabrics. (*This is general information—we suggest that you follow the instructions given on the dye color packages. See the "Sources" section on page 63 for dye companies.*)

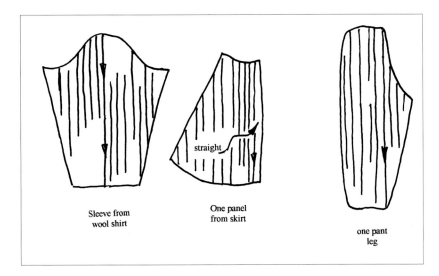

Sleeve from
wool shirt

One panel
from skirt

straight

one pant
leg

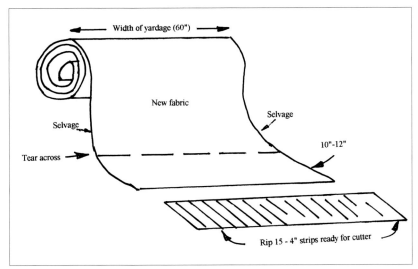

Width of yardage (60")

New fabric

Selvage

Selvage

Tear across

10"-12"

Rip 15 - 4" strips ready for cutter

The most important information to share before you start cutting is this: Be sure that you are cutting your strips on the **"straight of the goods."** Fabrics are woven with strong yarns going the length of the yardage. The filler yarns go from side to side (selvage to selvage).

Old clothes: Tearing is a perfect way for finding the "straight of the goods." Even though you may be timid of tearing, you will find that wool tears very well. Rip pieces about 2" wide; then do further cutting by hand.

Yardage: Notice the direction of the "straight of the goods." Now notice where the "selvage edges" are located. It is important to cut the fabric in this manner right at the start so that you don't lose sight of the "straight of the goods" of your fabric. Tear a 12" piece of fabric from the yard, from selvage to selvage. Now tear a 3" or 4" section from this 12" piece. You will know later that the 12" section is from the "straight of the goods," and the 3" or 4" piece is from selvage to selvage.

Cutting into strips: You can cut the fabric pieces in strips by hand as shown, or use a hooking cutter. (See the "Sources" section on page 63 for cutter dealers.)

BASIC HOOKING INSTRUCTIONS
by Happy and Steve DiFranza

Transferring a Pattern to Backing

Beginning rug hookers often have problems figuring out how to transfer a printed pattern (such as the 12 patterns in this book) onto a rug backing fabric (burlap, monk's cloth, etc.). There are several ways to go about it, but the first step in all cases is to decide how big you want your rug to be.

Once you've determined that, a pen, ruler, and a little arithmetic are needed for one transferring method. Draw a grid over the printed pattern. For a simple pattern the grid's squares can be large; for a complex one, make them small. Use the same number of squares to draw a grid on the rug backing. To achieve proper proportions, calculate the size of the squares. Say you want your rug to be a 40" square, and you've used 8 squares across the top of your printed pattern's grid. 40÷8=5, so that means your 8 squares on the backing should be 5" on each side. You also used 8 squares down the side of the pattern, so you'll also use eight, 5" squares along the side as well. This grid will allow you to draw fragments of the pattern in the correct spot and in the correct proportion.

Another method employs a copy machine and nylon veiling (available at fabric stores). After you've used the copier to enlarge the pattern to the desired size, tape the veiling over it and trace all the lines onto the veiling. (It helps to have a transparent ruler to get the lines perfectly straight.) Then tape the marked veiling onto the backing. Retrace the lines on the veiling with a felt-tip pen so they bleed through onto the backing.

An iron-on pattern pencil that makes an indelible blue line can also help you transfer. (The pencils are available through suppliers who advertise in *Rug Hooking*.) Tape tracing paper over the pattern. Using a light table or a sunny window, trace the design onto the tracing paper with an ordinary pencil; turn the tracing paper over and draw over the lines with the pattern pencil, making a mirror image of the design.

Set your iron on high (cotton setting) and allow it to heat up well. Place the tracing paper with the mirror image down on the backing. Holding the paper securely, iron slowly over the design. Press hard, and do not move the iron around the design. Lift and reposition

HOW TO HOLD *by Verna P. Cox*

1 Hold the fabric strip lightly in your left hand between thumb and forefinger (or in your right hand if you're left-handed).

2 Hold the hook as a pencil with hook facing up.

3 Insert the hook through backing fabric with the hook facing up.

Lean the hook back to create a wider hole in the backing fabric to allow you to bring the strip up more easily.

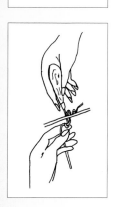

4 Notice in this drawing how the hook is positioned under the strand being held by the left hand. The first part of the strip is pulled all the way out to the top of the backing fabric. This strip will be cut to the proper length later. The loops are pulled up as evenly as possible. Try to go into each hole, but if the loops become too crowded, then you can skip a hole. When you get to the end of a strand, pull the end through to the top of the backing fabric. Now you can clip both the beginning and ending of the strip to the same height as the loops.

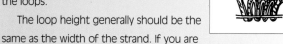

Cut ends even with tops of loops

The loop height generally should be the same as the width of the strand. If you are using a 1/8" strip, then the loops are pulled up 1/8". Most strips are cut about 12" long, but you can cut them any length you wish.

5 Notice how the beginning and ends of each strip are cut to create one smooth surface: This allows no strip ends left to the back of the rug where the strips could be pulled out.

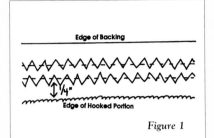

Figure 1

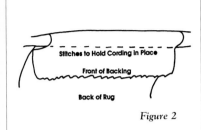

Figure 2

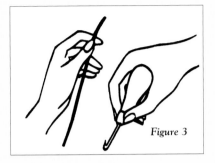

Figure 3

carefully until you have pressed the entire design. Be patient to allow enough time for the lines to be transferred onto the backing. (The pencil lines turn blue as they transfer.)

To check if the pattern has transferred successfully, lift a corner of the paper carefully so that it doesn't move. When all the lines are clearly visible on the burlap, it is ready.

Finish Before You Start

Finishing the edges of hooked pieces is critically important to improve their durability, particularly for floor rugs. When walked on for a number of years, poorly finished edges crack and split, requiring reconstruction that may be unsightly.

Unfortunately, even some experienced rug hookers do not finish their edges well. A quick review of common finishing techniques will benefit even the most seasoned rug hookers and may keep beginners from forming bad habits.

Before you begin hooking a pattern, machine stitch two rows around the perimeter as a defense against fraying. Stitch the first row $1/4$" beyond what will be the hooked portion, and the second row 1/4" beyond the first row ($1/2$" beyond the hooked portion). Overstitch each row of straight stitches with a row

of zigzag stitches as shown in **Figure 1.**

After hooking the entire rug, vacuum it lightly and check it for mistakes. Lay it on a sheet wrong-side up and cover it with a damp towel. Stamp press it lightly with a dry iron to flatten it; do not rub it as if ironing clothing. Rehook bulging or uneven areas before finishing the edges.

The finished edge should be as high as the hooking, so select cording accordingly. Use preshrunk, natural-fiber cording: clothesline, heavy twine, etc.

Fold the backing toward the backside of the rug, about $1/2$" from the hooked portion. Insert the cording and baste it into place with thread as shown in **Figure 2.** When whipped with yarn, the cording preserves the edge of the rug by taking the pressure of footsteps.

Dye woolen yarn to match your border or to coordinate with your color plan. After the cording is in place, whip the yarn around it with a blunt needle. You will use about one foot of yarn for each inch of whipping.

To whip the edge, simply sew yarn around the cording that is already covered with backing. Whip right up to the edge of the hooked portion on the front, out the back of the rug, around the cording, and down into the front again.

Continue around the perimeter of the rug, making sure the whipping covers the backing evenly. Do not start

at a corner. At the corners, you will need to whip more stitches to cover the backing, and you will not be able to create perfectly square corners.

On the backside of the rug, hand-stitch 1 $1/4$" cotton binding tape right up to the edge of the whipping. Miter the tape and the backing at the corners. Cut away the excess backing so the raw edge is hidden under the tape. Finally, sew the inner edge of the tape between loops in the back of the hooked portion to cover the raw edge of the backing.

Sew a label onto the back of your rug. Include your name and location, the name and dimensions of the rug, the designer, the date, and any other pertinent information. Give the rug one final steam press as described above, using a much wetter towel. Lay it flat to dry.

How to Hook

These basic instructions apply to hooking with all widths of woolen strips. Step 3, however, applies to hooking with narrow strips in #3, 4, and 5 cuts. (The number refers to the numerical designation of a cutter wheel on a fabric cutting machine. A #3 wheel cuts a strip $3/32$" wide; a #5 cuts a strip $5/32$" wide; a #8, $8/32$" or $1/4$" wide, and so on.) Refer to the section on hooking with wide strips for special tips on holding a hook when making a wide-cut rug.

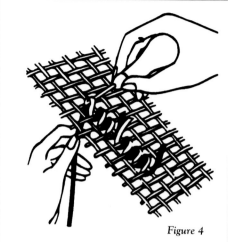

Figure 4

Figure 5

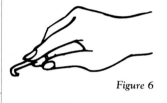

Figure 6

1 Stretch the backing in a hoop or frame with the design side up. Sitting comfortably, rest the hoop or frame on a table or your lap. The thumbscrew of a hoop should be opposite you.

2 With your left hand (right hand if you're a leftie) hold the end of a woolen strand between your thumb and forefinger **(Figure 3)**.

3 With your right hand, hold the hook as if it were a pencil, with your fingertips on the metal collar as shown.

4 Hold the wool in your left hand and put it beneath the backing. With your right hand, push the hook down through the mesh. The shaft of the hook should touch your left forefinger and slide behind the woolen strip. Push the wool onto the barb with your left thumb.

5 With the hook, pull the end of the strip through to the front of the backing with the hook, to a height of about $1/2$".

6 Push the hook down through the backing a little to the left of the strip's end and catch the strip underneath. Pull up a $1/8$" loop, or as high as

the strip is wide. To prevent pulling out the previous loop, lean the hook back toward the previous loop as you pull up another loop.

7 Working from right to left, make even loops that gently touch each other as in **Figure 4.** With fine strips, hook in almost every hole. Never put more than one loop in a hole.

8 When you reach the end of the woolen strip, pull the end up through the backing. Pull all ends through to the front as you hook. Tails on the back are untidy and can be easily pulled out.

9 Start the next strip in the same hole in which the last strip ended, again leaving a $1/2$" tail.

10 Trim the ends even with the loops after making several loops with the new strip.

11 Continue the hooking process until the pattern is complete. To keep the back of the rug from becoming lumpy, do not cross a row of hooking with another strip. Cut the strip and start again.

12 Practice the following exercises to achieve the proper rhythm and technique: (a) after hooking straight lines, try wavy lines; (b) pack rows against one another to form a pile as in **Figure 5.**

Even the most skilled rug hooker must pull out loops now and then. Individual strands can be removed easily, but loops in packed areas are harder to remove. Use the hook or a pair of tweezers. Strands may be re-used if they are not badly frayed, and the blank area of the backing may be hooked again.

Hooking with Wide Strips

When hooking with wide strips ($1/4$" to $1/2$"), note that they pull up more easily if you hold the hook in the palm of your hand **(Figure 6)** and insert it into the backing at a sharper angle. (Some even prefer to hold the hook in this manner when working with narrow strips.) As with narrow strips, the shaft of the hook should rub the forefinger of your left hand and pass behind the woolen strip. The barb should hit your thumb, which pushes the wool onto the hook. Never loop the wool over the hook with your left hand; this will result in a lumpy back. If you cannot pick up the strip with your hook, the barb is not properly positioned.—*Happy and Steve DiFranza*

WHERE TO START HOOKING

The order that most rug hookers follow is:

1 Outline the art objects (motifs).

2 Fill in the motifs.

3 Work in background around the motifs, and fill in most of the background.

4 Hook three to four rows of straight hooking around the entire outside edge of hooked piece.

5 Finish hooking the background.

METHODS OF FILLING IN MOTIFS OR BACKGROUNDS

The style you pick will depend on you and the art you are creating.

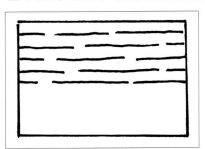

METHOD 1

Method #1 shows the hooking done in straight lines.

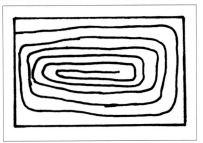

METHOD 2

Method #2 shows the hooking being done from the outside edge to the center.

METHOD 3

Method #3 shows how you can hook in oddly shaped sections for filling in background or motifs.

COLOR SHADING ART WORK

Even though shading is usually done in the process of traditional rug hooking rather than in primitive rugs, it doesn't mean you can't use shading with either style. The choice is entirely up to you. Here are two methods that can be used to add shading to your design.

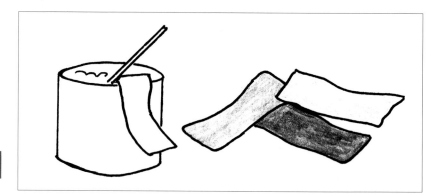

METHOD 1

Method #1: You can purchase or dye your own rectangular sections of fabric in shades of the color you need. The reason for the rectangular shape is that you always need to know the "straight of the fabric," and you will know that the longest dimension (usually 10" to 12") is always the straight of the goods. (Your hooking strips, as a result, will be 10" to 12" long.)

Notice how the colored pieces are dyed in shades to help you with your art design. If you are dyeing your own, you need to keep track of how much color you used and the name or names of the colors.

In the drawing, notice how the darkest shade on the leaf is hooked in a straight line around the object. Then, the next shade is used in another row to the inside of the first row. This method makes the leaf look more realistic.

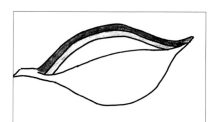

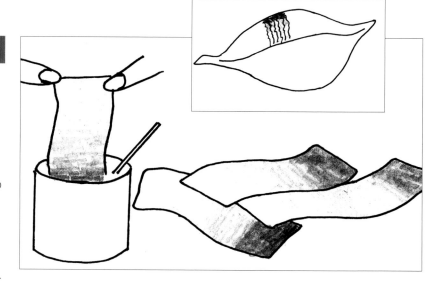

METHOD 2

Method #2: You can purchase or dye your own fabric pieces for this method. Remember to have the pieces of fabric cut in rectangular shapes so that you remember which length is the "straight of the goods." In this method of dyeing, the piece of fabric is dipped partway into the "dye bath," so that the lower part of the strip gets darker than the top.

In the illustration, the darkest end of the hooking strip is started at the edge of the leaf, and the hooking automatically becomes lighter and lighter toward the inside of the leaf. This contributes to an even more realistic look than you might achieve with Method #1.

FINISHING THE PROJECT

If you plan to use your rug in its present size and shape, here are a few methods:

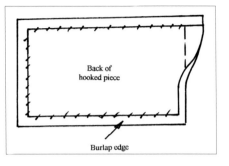

Back of hooked piece

Burlap edge

METHOD 1

Method #1: Turn the backing fabric hem over twice, and steam in place before securing it with fine stitches to the backing of the hooked piece.

METHOD 2

Method #2: Apply twill tape to the edge of the backing fabric as shown. The backing fabric should be cut about 1" from the hooking. Notice how the twill tape is stitched (either by hand or sewing machine) to the backing fabric as close to the hooking as is possible. Also notice that the twill tape is applied to the top of the hooked piece, then turned over. Press the twill tape in place, and secure with fine sewing stitches to the back of the hooked piece.

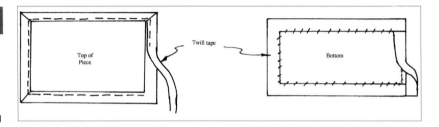

Top of Piece

Twill tape

Bottom

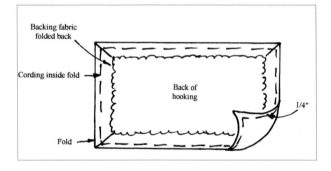

Backing fabric folded back

Cording inside fold

Back of hooking

1/4"

Fold

METHOD 3

Method #3: Iron back the backing fabric with steam iron and pressing cloth, leaving a space of $1/4$" between the border of the hooked piece and the crease in the backing. Within this crease, insert a cording, the size you feel needed for height of the hooking, and "whip" that edge (cording within backing) with a heavy-duty yarn or thread. This protects the hooked piece from wear. After the stitching has been done, then hand-stitch a piece of twill tape to the back of the rug. The tape overlaps the raw edge of the backing fabric.

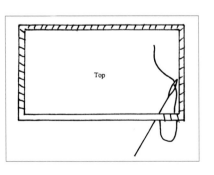

Top

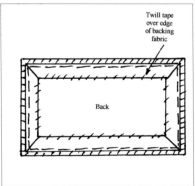

Twill tape over edge of backing fabric

Back

PREPARING PROJECT FOR BRAIDED BORDER

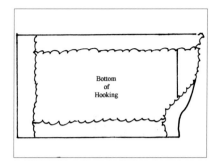
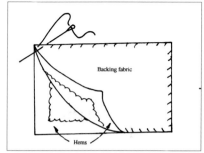
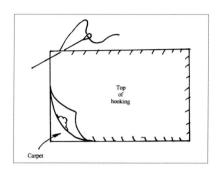

METHOD 1

Method #1: If you plan to use a fabric for the backing, place the ironed, hooked piece on top of the backing as a pattern, and cut the fabric at least 1" larger than the hooked piece. Turn in the 1" hem and press. Now with both top and lower pieces placed together (with hem sides facing each other) whipstitch the edge to hold both top and bottom layers together. Now you are ready to apply the first row of braiding. The sew/lace method is used only for the first row. With a pointed yarn needle, sew on the hooked piece, but then turn the needle and lace into the braid.

METHOD 2

Method #2: If you plan to use a light-weight "indoor/outdoor" carpeting (this increases the rug's durability for use out-doors) on the back of the rug, you need to first press the hem of the hooked piece to the back. Using this as a pattern, place your finished rug on the piece of carpet to be used as backing fabric.

With chalk or pen, trace the size of the rug onto the carpet and cut the carpet $1/16$" larger than the hooked piece. This is important to prevent wrinkling on the hooked piece later. Stitch both the layers (hooked piece and carpet) together with whipstitches

around the edge using a matching color thread. Now you are ready to apply your first row of braiding. The **sew/lace method** is used only for the first row. With a pointed yarn needle, sew onto the edge of the hooked piece, turn needle, and lace with eye end of the needle into the braid.

For more information on rug braiding, be sure to see my pamphlet and video on braiding. (See the "Sources" section on page 63 for more information on all Verna's products.)

SEW/LACE METHOD

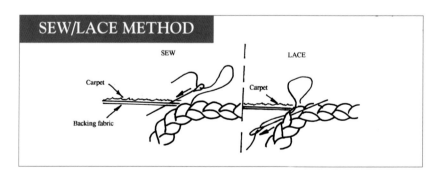

HELPFUL HOOKING HINTS

1 Usually the motifs in your design are hooked first by outlining them, then filling them in.

2 Then work on the background from the center to the finished edge.

3 Before filling in the entire background, jump ahead to create three to four smooth rows of hooking all around the outer edge of the piece. Then fill in the rest of the background. This method allows you to have a smoother edge to your hooked piece.

4 While working on the background, decide what method you plan to use based on the motifs you are creating. If you are doing a sky, perhaps you may want straight lines. If it is a one-color background, you may want to do the hooking in oddly shaped sections to add visual interest. The decision is based on you and your design.

5 When trying to hook in a curved line, you will find it easier if you move the lower strip (that is held in your left hand under the backing) in the direction you want to go first before hooking with the hook in that direction.

6 If you are having problems with the fabric splitting, you may be doing two things. One, you may have cut the fabric on the bias, instead of on the straight. Second, you may not be "laying" your hook under the lower fabric strip. If the hook is held straight up instead of like a pencil, you may be catching only part of the lower strip. Notice how the hook "lays" under the lower strip.

7 If you are having a problem with previous loops pulling down as you are creating a new loop, you may be holding the lower strip (with your left hand) too tightly. You need only to guide the lower strip, not hold it firmly.

8 Usually strips for hooking are cut 10" to 12" long, but you can cut the pieces any length you wish.

9 In working on a pattern or a background, remember that when you get to the end of a row of hooking, it may be easier to end that strip there, by cutting and pulling the end to the top, instead of turning your hoop around to continue with the same strip.

10 Do yourself a favor and start collecting old clothes to have as a source of special tweeds and plaids for certain parts of your designs. Yard sales are good for this. All of the garments should be washed and pre-shrunk so that the hooking strips will be stronger.

Verna P. Cox teaches rug hooking and rug braiding in Verona Island, Maine. For more information on all of Verna's products, as well as complete ordering information, see the "Sources" section on page 63 of this book.

WHAT IS RUG HOOKING?

Some strips of wool. A simple tool. A bit of burlap. How ingenious were the women and men of ages past to see how such humble household items could make such beautiful rugs?

Although some form of traditional rug hooking has existed for centuries, this fiber craft became a fiber art only in the last 150 years. The fundamental steps have remained the same: A pattern is drawn onto a foundation, such as burlap or linen. A zigzag line of stitches is sewn along the foundation's edges to keep them from fraying as the rug is worked. The foundation is then stretched onto a frame, and fabric strips or yarn, which may have been dyed by hand, are pulled through it with an implement that resembles a crochet hook inserted into a wooden handle. The compacted loops of wool remain in place without knots or stitching. The completed rug may have its edges whipstitched with cording and yarn as a finishing touch to add durability.

Despite the simplicity of the basic method, highly intricate designs can be created with it. Using a multitude of dyeing techniques to produce unusual effects, or various hooking methods to create realistic shading, or different widths of wool to achieve a primitive or formal style, today's rug hookers have gone beyond making strictly utilitarian floor coverings to also make wallhangings, vests, lampshades, purses, pictorials, portraits, and more. Some have incorporated other kinds of needlework into their hooked rugs to fashion unique and fascinating fiber art that's been shown in museums, exhibits, and galleries throughout the world.

For a good look at what contemporary rug hookers are doing with yesteryear's craft—or to learn how to hook your own rug—pick up a copy of *Rug Hooking* magazine, or visit our web site at *www.rughookingonline.com*. Within the world of rug hooking—and *Rug Hooking* magazine—you'll find there's a style to suit every taste and a growing community of giving, gracious fiber artists who will welcome you to their gatherings.—*Wyatt R. Myers*

by Cherylyn Brubaker

Appliqué Flower Basket

A ppliqué *Flower Basket* was designed with beginning rug hookers in mind. New hooking students are often drawn to large rug patterns, but finishing a smaller project first can be a satisfying way to learn the basics before investing a lot of time and money.

The color scheme of *Appliqué Flower Basket* is muted. I have selected rusty peach tones for the flowers, although burgundy and rose would also work. The stems and leaves are light, medium (plaid), and dark olive-green. Two plaids—a light brown and a dark brown—form the basket. For the background I used a Joan Moshimer formula (see the sidebar) to simulate onion-skin dyeing. I used this formula instead of onion skins to create a consistent background color for kits I was preparing, which is why I'm presenting it here. But one of the easiest methods of dyeing is with onion skins.

There are several reasons to learn to dye your own wool: I find that it is becoming increasingly difficult to find wool in certain colors; commercially dyed wool is flat in appearance and not as interesting as hand-dyed wool; and recycled wool often needs to be toned down or enhanced. By dyeing your wool, even if it is only with onion skins, you will give your hooked rugs a richness only hand-dyed wool can impart. As an example, I used onion skins to dye some bright wools we would normally avoid, as well as some pastels (see the photos). The result is lovely, related hues.

Onion-Skin Dyeing

Dyeing wool with onion skins can be done using regular kitchen utensils,

FABRIC REQUIREMENTS

BACKGROUND:
- 1/2 yard of natural or old ivory wool, dyed with onion skins or with Joan Moshimer's formula (see below)

BASKET AND BORDER:
- 12" x 18" piece of light brown plaid (also used for flowers)
- 12" x 18" piece of dark brown plaid

LEAVES:
- 5" x 18" piece of light olive-green wool
- 10" x 18" piece of medium olive-green (solid or plaid) for flower stems, veins, and border
- 6" x 18" piece of dark olive-green

FLOWERS:
- 9" x 18" piece of light peach wool (also used in border)
- 4" x 18" piece of dark peach

JOAN MOSHIMER'S FORMULA
(Cushing dyes)
- 1/4 tsp Ecru
- 1/4 tsp Old Ivory
- 1/4 tsp Champagne

Dissolve the dyes in 1 cup of boiling water. (Put the dyes in a 1-cup glass measure and add a few teaspoons of tepid water to form a paste. Add boiling water to the 1-cup level and stir it briskly until the dyes are dissolved completely.) Use 1/2 cup of the solution to dye 1/2 yard of natural ivory wool.

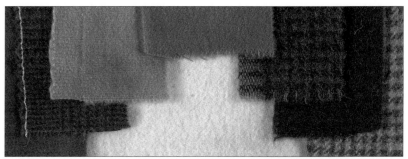

Samples of the wool Cherylyn used to hook her Appliqué Flower Basket.

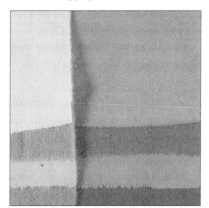

Cherylyn used onion-skin dyeing to transform the pastel wools on the left into the related hues on the right.

The bright wools on the left were toned down with onion-skin dyeing to yield the muted colors on the right.

Appliqué Flower Basket, *16 1/4" x 13", #6- and 7-cut wool on linen. Designed and hooked by Cherylyn Brubaker, Brunswick, Maine, 1998.*

unlike acid reactive dyeing, which requires equipment that is never used for food preparation. Onion-skin dyeing is also inexpensive because you use something you would normally throw away.

Net bags that the onions themselves come in are actually perfect for storing onion skins. Hanging the bag allows the air to circulate through it, drying the skins further. Save the outer hard brown skins from yellow or white onions (not red ones). If you or your family are not onion eaters, your local grocer will probably let you collect the loose skins that accumulate in the onion bin.

The first requirement for dyeing is a dye solution. Stuff a clean, knee-high nylon full of onion skins, and knot the end. Fill a 4-quart pan with 5 cups of water; add the stocking full of onion skins; and place the pan over medium heat. When the solution is nearly boiling, turn the heat down to a simmer and cook the skins for 90 minutes. A golden red-brown color will gradually be released from the onion skins—this will be your dye solution. To overdye strong colors or a lot of yardage, increase the amount of stuffed stockings and water.

Meanwhile, soak 1/2 yard of natural wool in warm water and a wetting agent such as Synthrapol or Wetter than Wet, or a small amount of dish-washing soap. Saturated wool will absorb dye more easily and evenly. If you desire a more antique background for *Appliqué Flower Basket*, begin with wool that is not as white, such as light taupe or old ivory.

Because the background needed for *Appliqué Flower Basket* is fairly light in color, add your solution judiciously. The dye produced by the onion skins is more like a stain. Too much will produce not a glow, but an orange tone. It is far easier to add more color than to take it out.

Add 4" to 5" of water to an 8-quart pot. Add more water if you desire a smooth, even color to your wool; less if you want a splotchy look. Pour the dye solution into a 1-cup measuring cup. Start by adding 1/4 cup of the solution to the pot, then the wet wool. Using tongs or while wearing heavy, lined rubber gloves, move the wool around so the dye is distributed over the whole piece and heat it slowly over medium heat until the water clears.

If the color is too light when the water clears, remove the wool, add more solution, and return the wool to the pot. (Keep in mind that when wet, wool is at least one shade darker than when dry.) When the wool is the color you want, add ¹/₂ cup of white vinegar to the pot and simmer the wool for 20 minutes. Carefully put the dyed wool in a sink and rinse out the vinegar, going from hot to cooler water. Save leftover onion-skin solution in your refrigerator or freeze it, labeled, for future use. If your pot is stained after dyeing, clean it with bleach or scouring cleanser.

Preparing the Pattern

Decide what kinds of backing you want to use for your *Appliqué Flower Basket* (I used linen), remembering that you will hook this project in a #6 cut of wool. I cheated a little because the background is not my favorite thing to hook, so I used a #7 cut for it. When I jumped to a larger cut, I first hooked a row of #6-cut background wool around the basket, flowers, and leaves, then filled in the rest of the background with #7-cut wool. If you prefer, you can hook the whole piece in a #6 cut.

First read the transferring, hooking, and finishing instructions that begin on page 8. Then enlarge the pattern on page 19 to 16 ¹/₄" x 13"

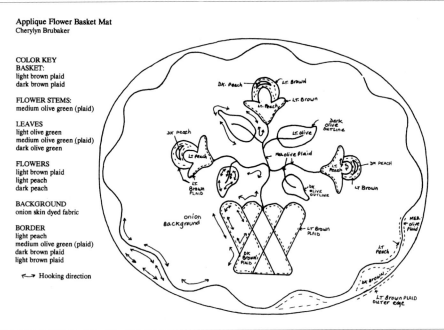

and transfer it to your backing material. Leave at least 3" to 4" of material around the design and align the pattern on the straight of the fabric. Make sure to use a permanent marker to transfer the pattern to the backing.

How to Hook *Appliqué Flower Basket*

Hooking direction is always important, but it takes on even more emphasis when using wider cuts of wool because every loop shows. Textured wool loops, however, are less obvious than those of solid fabric. On this piece I used contour hooking to fill in the motifs, background, and border. This means my hooking followed the shapes of the basket, flowers, leaves, and border. (The diagram above shows the hooking directions for this project.)

Begin by outlining the basket with light brown plaid wool. Hook right on the lines to ensure a straight basket. Fill in the shape with dark brown wool, following the contours.

Next hook the wavy stems, hooking right on the lines with medium olive-green. Use the same wool to hook the leaf veins. Outline the leaves using the darkest olive and fill them in with light olive. Hook the leaves and flowers just inside the lines to avoid making the motifs too large.

Hook with light brown plaid along the bottom edge of each flower and then use light peach to fill the large portion of the blossom. As you hook the curves, maintain an even height with your loops. Outline the top crescent of the flower using light brown plaid and fill the inside of the crescent with dark peach.

It is a good habit to hook some of the background as you go. Outline each motif with the background color to define its shape and fill in the background around the flower stems and leaves.

If you wish to apply the binding tape by machine, do it now. Place one edge of the tape against the pattern, and outline and sew a double line of stitching close to the edge of the

binding. Then sew a double row of zigzag stitching on the backing about 1/2" past the outside border to prevent fraying. If you wish to sew the binding on by hand, do it after you've completed the hooking.

To put your initials on your mat, use a permanent marker to draw them on the pattern below the basket. Use the light brown plaid to hook the letters, then hook around them with background wool.

Now complete the border. Hook a row of light peach inside the wavy line (see diagram on page 18), then a row of medium olive-green outside it. Place one row of light brown plaid on the outer edge of the pattern. Fill in the border with dark brown. Hook the remaining background with onion-skin dyed wool.

Check the back of your mat for "holidays"—places you may have missed. Fix them by pulling out a strand and rehooking it one or two threads over or by filling in with another strip. This is where those too thin pieces you've cut come in handy. If you have a hard time finding the spots when you've turned the mat over, poke toothpicks through from the back to mark those places.

Trim the backing just outside the row of zigzag stitching. Turn the binding tape to the back and stitch it into place by hand.

Steaming will help take out bumps and minimize differences in loop height. I like to lightly steam-press a project before I do the finishing because any problem areas will then be obvious. After the finishing is complete, I do a final pressing, laying the mat on a towel, hooked side up, until it is dry.

Congratulations! I'll bet your *Appliqué Flower Basket* looks terrific.

Cherylyn Brubaker sells her patterns through her mail-order business, Hooked Treasures, 6 Iroquois Circle, Brunswick, ME 04011, (207) 729-1380. Appliqué Flower Basket is available as a pattern or kit.

by Jane Olson

The Barn

Years ago, primitive rug patterns often featured objects around the home, including the house itself. The materials that were available were cut by hand and used as is to create colorful pictorials. We have come a long way with our commercial patterns, specialty dyed wool, and cloth-stripping machines, but the motifs are still fun to hook.

I always think of primitives as rural designs, and this pattern certainly falls into that category. This pattern can be hooked traditionally with a #4 cut, but the directions that follow are for hooking the pattern with a #5 or 6 cut of wool.

Fabric Possibilities

The Barn measures 30" x 20", or 4½ square feet. It requires 2 to 3 pounds of wool. Your scrap bag will be a wonderful source of materials. The following amounts of materials are mostly spot dyed or mottled using Cushing dyes, but use your own judgment and imagination. If you have a lot of odds and ends of swatches in the same color family, mix and match them and use them for the barn, trees, grass, and so on. You can use solids, checks, or tweeds; the more variety you use, the more interesting the pictorial will be. There is room for lots of variety in choice of color as well; following is the color plan I used for the rug as shown on page 21.

Color and Amounts of Wool

Here are the colors and amounts of wool you will need to hook *The Barn*.

■ **Sky:** ⅓ yard white or natural wool

EXCLUSIVE DESIGN: *See the "Exclusive Designs" section after page 32 for a large pull-out pattern of this rug!*

overdyed with Cushing's Sky Blue or Light Blue. To add visual interest, this can be spot dyed with a little Silver Gray and Violet.

■ **Trees and bushes:** ½ yard of white, natural, or green wool, spot dyed with Bronze Green, a little Reseda Green, and Gold. If you would like your version to depict more of a fall scene, spot dye using more Gold and Rust.

■ **Roof of barn and silo, outlining, background of stone foundation, and border background:** 1 yard of as-is gray check or tweed, or white overdyed with Cushing's Slate Gray or Gray. This wool can be dyed by placing the material in the dye bath and not stirring it during the setting time.

■ **Hill and grass in forefront of picture:** ½ yard beige wool spot dyed with Gold, Taupe, and Bronze Green. You can vary the amounts of dye that you use. If you prefer a summer scene,

use more of the Bronze Green. If you want a fall scene, use more of the Gold and Taupe.

■ **Fence posts, stone in barn foundation:** ¼ yard beige or tan wool spot dyed with Silver Gray, Taupe, and Medium Brown. Dye two shades to be used for the light and dark sides of the posts.

■ **Barn and silo:** ⅜ yard of white, beige, natural, or pastel pink wool, overdyed with Cushing's Turkey Red in three mottled shades—a light shade for the sunlit side, a medium shade for the dark side, and a very dark shade for the separation between the boards.

■ **Trunks of trees, ramp to the barn:** ⅛ yard of Brown or Taupe spot-dyed tweed or check. This can also be used for highlights in the road.

■ **Road, furrowed ground:** ⅛ yard of beige or tan wool, spot dyed with Medium Brown and Taupe.

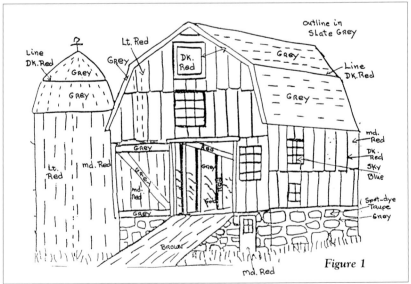

Figure 1

The Barn,
30" x 20",
#6-cut wool
on burlap.
Designed
and hooked
by Jane
Olson,
Inglewood,
California,
1995.

Hooking Your Pictorial

Start your hooking with the barn. Outline the building, windows, and doors in Slate Gray, then hook the barn walls vertically, using the lightest red shade for the front of the barn and the medium shade for the side. Use the darkest red shade for the spaces between the boards. Hook the roof with gray, working horizontally. Use Sky Blue for the windows and Slate Gray for their frames.

Hook the silo in the same manner, but follow the contours when hooking the gray roof (see Figure 1 on page 20). Use the darkest shade of red for the line in the roof of the barn and silo.

When hooking the tree leaves, hook in the direction of the contours of the leaf bunches (see Figure 2 below). Whether you are using spot-dyed wool or swatches, hook them in the same way. Then hook the tree trunks vertically with the brown tweed or check material. Use this same wool for the lines in the furrowed ground.

The mailbox is optional. I would hook it in red with a gray flag. Hook the post it sits on in the same way as the fence posts: Hook one side with a light spot dye and the other side with a dark spot dye.

The barbed wire between the posts in the border is a light spot dye. This will show up well against the slate gray background. Hook the barbed wire between the fence posts in the picture with Slate Gray.

When hooking the grass areas, follow the contours as shown in Figure 2. Hook the long grass vertically. Follow the directions of the furrows when hooking the plowed field.

Hook the narrow outside border with two rows of dark red. Also hook one row of dark red between the picture and the wide border.

Follow the road's contours when hooking it (see Figure 3 below). Hook the lines first with the tweed or check material used for the tree trunks. Fill in the rest of the area with the medium brown and taupe spot dyes. A mixture of brown, beige, and taupe spot dyes works well for the road. Outline the road with Slate Gray.

Use Slate Gray again for the inside of the barn, and gold and brown for the hay stacked inside. Hook the hay bin posts with red.

Fill in any other details with compatible colors. You may want to draw a few farm animals here and there to add to the pastoral scene.

Jane Olson is a member of our editorial board. This pattern is available from her rug studio at PO Box 351, Hawthorne, California 90250, (310) 643-5902.

Figure 2

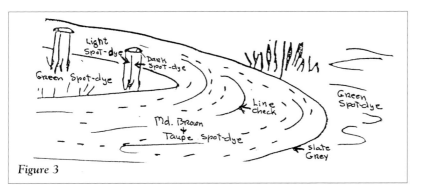

Figure 3

by Anne Ashworth

Beginner's Rose

If you are a beginning rug hooker, you may feel intimidated by the prospect of shading, especially if you've had no instruction in it. This simple rose is what I use to teach all my beginning students the basics of hooking and shading. It is a typical cup-and-saucer rose, in which the outside petals form the saucer and the upright petals the cup. The shading is done with six values, from the lightest (#1) to the darkest (#6). Five leaves surround the rose for color and balance, although the two back leaves can be omitted.

Prepare the Pattern

To hook this simple rose, first you must prepare your pattern. For your backing you may use fine burlap, monk's cloth, or fabric that does not need to be hooked, such as the polyester I used for my *Beginner's Rose* on page 24. Use a piece of backing measuring at least 16" square.

Copy or trace the pattern on page 26 onto a piece of paper. There are two effective methods for transferring the design from the paper to the backing. The first is to trace the design on netting or bridal veiling. Along with the design also mark the corners of the paper on the veiling; they'll serve as a guide when you center the pattern on the backing. Then place the netting over the backing. Go over the design (but not the corner marks) on the netting with a permanent marker, and the lines will bleed through to the backing.

Anne used Dorr's Potpourri swatches in Woodrose and Grey Green to hook her Beginner's Rose.

The second transfer method is to tape the pattern to a sunny window and then tape your backing over it. You should be able to see through the backing enough to trace the design. Use a waterproof laundry-marking pen, but beware. Some waterproof ink has bled when I've steam-pressed the finished piece.

If you are an absolute beginner and are not sure if you will continue with hooking, do not go to the expense of purchasing a lot of fancy equipment. An inexpensive crochet hook will work fine for the hooking. Use a 12"

embroidery hoop for your hooking frame. I found I could balance the hoop on the edge of a table and hold it down with a heavy book. You can even frame the finished picture in the hoop, as I've done. If you're going to do that, take the hoop apart and make sure that each piece of it has no noticeable flaws.

Hooking the Rose

To complete the rose you will need two 3" x 12" six-value swatches—one red (or rose) and one green. Many suppliers carry wool that is dyed in graded swatches. You can also purchase it cut into strips. (I used Dorr Potpourri swatches in Woodrose and Grey Green, cut into #3 strips, for my *Beginner's Rose*.)

If you have some experience dyeing and would like to dye your own wool, try overdyeing red fabric (wash it first, because the color runs) with $3/32$ teaspoon of Cushing Dark Green dye. For the leaves, dye yellow or pale blue wool with Dark Green. Use the undyed fabric for your first value; then dye five succeeding values according to the dyeing method you prefer.

Arrange the cut wool for the rose in sequence, so that value 6, then 5, 4, 3, 2, and 1 are in order. Refer to Figure 1 for the value placement in petals A through E.

Read the hooking instructions before you start to hook. Begin with the front petal lettered A. Pull your loops up as high as your strip is wide. Begin with value 6 and hook two rows

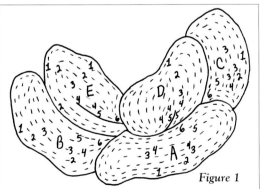

Figure 1

ILLUSTRATIONS BY ANNE ASHWORTH

Beginner's Rose, *12" in diameter, #3-cut wool on polyester. Designed and hooked by Anne Ashworth, Randolph Center, Vermont, 1999.*

along the back edge of the petal. Then cut that strand off and hook two rows of value 5. Those are the two shadow colors. Next place two rows of value 1 around the outer edge of the petal, then two rows of value 2 next to value 1. Those are the two highlight rows. Now hook value 3 next to 2, and value 4 next to 5. If this does not fill in the middle of the petal, add more of value 3 or 4. These two middle values create a transition between the highlight and shadow colors.

Hook petal B in the same manner as petal A, but note that the right side of the petal is under petal A, so use value 6 along that edge. Then hook petal C similarly. The left and bottom edges of petal C are under petals A and D and therefore need to be hooked with value 6.

Petals D and E are the beginning of the cup. Note the pattern line inside petal D. Hook a short piece of value 5 on that line, then a row of value 4 around it. Place three rows of value 1 on the outer edge, and then use values 2 and 3 to fill in the center. This petal should appear lighter than petal A.

Now hook petal E, starting with a line of value 6 right next to the outer edge of petal D. Then place one row of value 5 on the line in the center of the petal. Hook value 2 along the edge of petal E where it overlaps petal B and use two or three rows of value 1 for the rest of the outer edge. Then place a row of value 4 around the line you hooked with value 5. Hook a row or two of value 3 around 4; then use value 2 to continue to fill in the petal and meet the light edge.

Petals F through J are illustrated in Figure 2 on page 25. The two center petals (F and G) are very dark, using lots of value 6. Petal F has one row of value 1 and one row of value 2. Use values 3, 4, and 5 to fill in the petal to the base. Petal G is behind E and F, so it is also dark and only values 2, 3, 4, and 5 are used to fill it in. Pull a few threads from green and yellow wool and squeeze a few loops of each into the dark area in spots to suggest seeds.

Next hook petal H. Place one row of value 1 on the outer edge and then one row of 2 next to it. Fill in the rest of the petal with value 3, then 4, and then 5. Place a row of value 6 at the edge where it meets petals G and E. Hook petal I in a similar manner. On petal J use value 1 only on the two bumps on the outer edge of the petal. Hook the rest of the petal with the darker values—3, 4, 5, and 6—and place a few loops of value 2 next to 1.

The Leaves

Once you've completed the rose, you're ready to move on to the leaves. Figure 3 shows you the placement of values. Start with the right-hand leaf and hook its vein with value 2 of the green swatch. The base of the leaf is under the front edge of the rose, so you will need to hook it in the darkest value. Using value 6, hook a row along the edge of the rose and down to the middle of the vein. Then hook value 5 beside value 6 and continue with it to the tip of the vein. Fill in on both sides of the vein with value 5, then 4 around that, and then use value 3 to fill in the rest of the leaf. Add a few loops of value 2 along the left edge of the leaf. The tip of the leaf may also have one row of value 2 added.

The left-handed leaf overlaps the middle leaf, so the right-hand side of it will have to be light. Begin by hooking the vein in value 2. Hook only one row of value 6 at the base of the leaf and around the bottom branches of the vein. Then add one row of value 5 around the rest of the

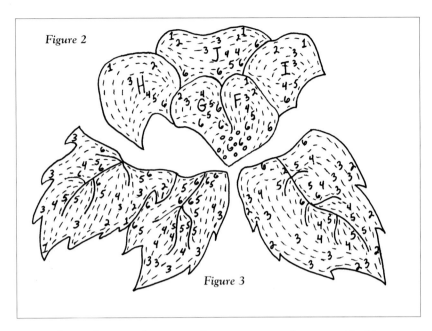

Figure 2

Figure 3

vein. Fill in with two or three rows of value 4 and then 3. Hook the right-hand side of the leaf with one row of value 3 and then one row of value 1 at the edge. If this does not fill the leaf completely, add some value 2 between values 1 and 3.

The middle leaf must be dark on the left side and all around the vein, which is hooked with value 2. Hook value 6 at the base of the leaf, along the left edge, and along both sides of the vein to its middle. Then use value 5 along the rest of the vein and around value 6. Fill in the rest of the leaf with values 4 and 5. Add a row of value 3 along the right edge and the tip of the leaf.

If you have included the two back leaves, you should have enough green wool left to hook them using value 2 for the veins and value 6 all around the veins. Fill them in with value 5 and then 4 on their outer edges.

Finishing and Framing

To finish your project, remove it from the embroidery hoop and carefully

steam-press the wrong side. Use a blind stitch to sew it onto a ready-made pillow top, or finish it as a picture as I did. To use the embroidery hoop as its frame, follow these steps. After pressing it, place the hooking back in the hoop and use a pencil to draw a line on the front side of the backing where it sticks out from the hoop. When you remove the hoop, you will see a crease from the hoop and a pencil line beyond it. With the hooking right side up, place white glue in the space between the crease and the line on the material. (Place aluminum foil under the material to keep from gluing it to the surface that you're working on.)

Allow the glue to dry for 24 hours. To make sure the picture stays in the hoop, add a little more glue between the line and the crease. Carefully center the inner part of the hoop under the picture, then place the outer hoop on top. The tricky part is putting the outer hoop on the picture without smearing the glue on everything. Pull the material as tight as it was when

you were hooking. Before tightening the hoop, make sure the picture is straight. When the glue has dried, trim the edges of the material close to the hoop. You can also clip the corners off the backing and blind stitch a lining over the back of the hoop.

Now that you've completed this simple shaded rose, you can move on to more complex projects. The best way to learn to shade is simply by doing it—a lot. Remember, we were all beginners once.

The fiber art of rug hooking lost an amazing artist, teacher, and friend when Anne Ashworth passed away in August 2001. Her lasting legacy of the Green Mountain Rug School and her pattern line, Green Mountain Hooked Rugs, lives on through her daughter, Stephanie Ashworth Krauss. All of Anne's original designs, as well as new designs, are available from Stephanie: 146 Main Street, Montpelier, VT 05602, vtpansy@ together.net. A kit for Beginner's Rose, containing the pattern, wool, a hoop, and a hook, is available from the Dorr Mill Store, PO Box 88, Guild, NH 03754, (800) 846-DORR.

by Jacqueline Hansen

**With a lesson on
adding fringe**

Chinese Peony

The traditional Oriental rug, with its jewel palette, elegant design, ethnic variations—and high price tag—could be called the Mercedes Benz of carpets. In borrowing these designs for hooked pieces, hookers use different techniques from those who create the tied and knotted rugs common in Asia.

Must you be a veteran rug hooker to embark on such a project? Not at all. In fact, a small Oriental design makes a good learning project for a beginner.

That's who I had in mind when I designed *Chinese Peony*, a modest 22" x 21" project that includes 2" of fringe on the short ends of the rug. Only a few values are used in the motifs so there is little shading, and this simplifies the work. The project also gives the beginner experience in shading within an outline and the use of #3 or #4 cuts of wool frequently used in Orientals to achieve a woven look.

Rugs of the Ming Dynasty were given an antique wash for an aged appearance. Keeping this in mind, I recommend soft, subdued colors for this piece. Using PRO Chem dyes, I

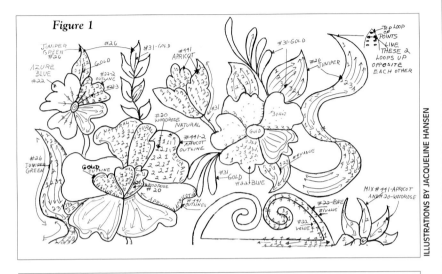

Figure 1

Figure 2

dyed my wool swatches in apricot, soft rose, aqua-blue, jade-green, and deep blue. You can achieve similar results by using Dorr Mill's Potpourri series of swatches, in particular Azure Blue, Apricot, Woodrose, and Juniper.

Apricot Swatches

Juniper Swatches

Azure Blue Swatches

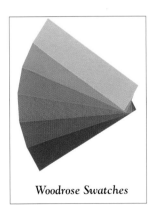

Woodrose Swatches

Chinese Peony, *22" x 21", #3- and 4-cut wool on burlap. Designed and hooked by Jacqueline Hansen, Scarborough, Maine, 1989.*

How to Hook
Chinese Peony

Before beginning to hook this rug, read all the instructions thoroughly. Pay particular attention to the directions for machine stitching the edges that begin on page 9; this should be done before you pull up your first loop. Also refer to the material sidebar on page 29 for the quantity and colors of wool you will need.

Included within this article is the pattern for *Chinese Peony*, as well as three figures, called value charts. The numbers in the figures refer to the values of the hues you should hook in certain areas. Value 6 is the darkest value; value 1 is the lightest.

Hook the flower petals as shown in Figure 1 on page 27. (Use a #4 cut throughout.) Begin with the largest lotus flower and outline the small center petals with Gold. Fill in these petals with value 1 and 2 of Woodrose wool, following the shape and contour of the petals. Finish the edges with one row of Natural wool directly next to the outline row of Gold, keeping the rows as close together as possible.

Outline the larger outside petals with value 2 of Apricot and shade the rest with the light values of Woodrose. Hook one row of Natural next to the Apricot outline. Starting in the center of the bud with value 2 of Apricot, hook the remainder with values of Apricot.

The sprays of leaves are hooked with gold, as are the veins and stems of the leaves. Hook the leaves with the light values of Juniper. To create the shape and twist for the ribbons, use values 1, 2, 3, and 4 of Juniper. Make sharp points for the tips of the leaves by hooking a single loop at the top of the tip, then, two loops underneath it and next to each other (see Figure 1).

See Figures 1 and 2 to hook the other large flowers. They are hooked in Azure Blue wool with Gold centers.

For the small flowers at the bottom of the rug (see Figures 2 and 3), vary your colors as shown. The color plan calls for two Woodrose flowers, one Apricot and one Azure Blue in this part of the rug, all of which tie your color plan together.

28

Figure 3

Now hook the center of the design—the *shou* motif. Use two rows of value 1 of Azure Blue and finish with one row of value 4 of Azure Blue to complete all the lines in this section.

Moving on to the border, hook two rows of Natural and one row of value 4 of Azure Blue as shown in Figure 3 on the right. For the small flowers in the border, hook values 1 and 2 of Apricot with a Gold center. Hook the leaves and ribbons in the border with values 1 and 2 of Juniper.

After each flower, leaf, and ribbon is outlined and filled, hook a row of Azure Blue, value 5, around each element. This row holds the shape of the motif and establishes the rich blue background color. Integrating the darkest values (5 and 6) of Azure Blue in the background will produce a hand-woven appearance. After completing the outlining, hook the background straight across the rows.

Hook the outer background of the border with three rows of value 6 of Azure Blue. This will give your completed hooking a neat, attractive look.

Adding Fringe and Finishing Edges

For a beautiful (and impressive) finish, crochet a fringe of Persian yarn at each short end of your rug. Overcast (whip) the longer sides of the rug with a yarn that matches the outer blue in the hooking. This finishing will add years to the life of your heirloom Oriental.

To overcast the edges, trim any excess backing that is beyond the line

MATERIALS

Here are the Dorr Mill Potpourri swatches you will need to hook *Chinese Peony*:
* **#100 Natural:** 1/2 yard
* **#20 Woodrose:** three 3" x 12" pieces of values 1 and 2
* **#441 Apricot:** Three 3" x 12" pieces of values 1 and 2
* **#31 Gold:** Two 3" x 12" pieces of value 4
* **#26 Juniper:** Four 3" x 12" pieces of values 1, 2, 3, and 4
* **#22 Azure Blue:** Three 3" x 12" pieces of values 1, 2, and 3
* **#22 Azure Blue:** Twelve 3" x 12" pieces of value 4, 1/2 yard of value 5; 1/2 yard of value 6

To finish the edges of the rug you will need:
* 1 skein of natural Persian wool yarn to crochet edges
* 1 skein of blue Persian yarn (match with Azure Blue) or 2 skeins to overcast all four edges
* 2 1/2 yards of matching dark blue cotton rug tape
* 2 1/2 yards of pillow cording

of machine stitching that you sewed before you began to hook. Baste or pin the backing, leaving 1/2" of fabric showing beyond the last row of hooking. Miter the corners.

Match the background color of your rug with tapestry or Persian yarn and overcast or whip all four sides (or only two if you are adding fringe), covering the pillow cording. Stitches should be as close together as possible, connecting with the first row of hooking. This process will cover the 1/2" of bare fabric, giving a strong, neat edge to the rug. If, over the years, the edge wears out, it is quite easy to repair it, provided you have kept a supply of yarn for mending.

Now turn your attention to the short edges of your rug. With white or ecru three-ply Persian yarn, begin single crochet stitches as close to the edge of the hooking as possible. Using your hook, chain three loops of yarn.

29

With your hook still in a loop, insert the hook through the fabric at the last row of hooking. Pull up the yarn as though you were hooking, making two loops on the hook. Next, cross the yarn over and pull the loop through the two loops already on your hook. This is a single crochet.

Continue this stitch until you reach the end of the rug. Try to judge your work so the crocheted edge will lie flat. Tie off and cut the yarn.

Decide the length of fringe you want and cut pieces of yarn so they are double that length. Take three or four of the cut pieces of yarn and fold them in half. Hold the yarn between your thumb and index finger, and with your hook in the opposite hand, insert the yarn in the first hole of the chain stitch. Catch the yarn at the fold. Pull the yarn through the chain hole and make a lasso. Continue to fill each hole, being careful to make the fringe lie flat. If the fringe appears too full, simple remove a strand.

Conversely, add a strand if it looks too skimpy. For this process you can work with or without the right side of the rug facing you, depending on which side of the lasso you prefer to have on top.

Jacqueline Hansen owns Jacqueline Designs in Scarborough, Maine. She sells the Chinese Peony pattern on verel (polyester panel cloth) in both a 20" x 21" and 30" x 42" size. Call her at (207) 883-5403.

by Jeanne Smith and Pat Brooks

Christmas Stocking

With a lesson on color planning

In November the crispness of the air stimulates our minds, and we begin to catch a little holiday spirit. We can already visualize wrapped packages under a decorated tree and handmade Christmas stockings hanging from the mantle before a warm fire. A quick look at the calendar foresees plenty of time to organize and bring these ideas to life. Yet past experiences remind us that our empty calendars will begin to fill quickly with social engagements, shopping trips, and visits from friends and family. Then panic sets in. When will there be time to recreate this festive setting? Relax! One solution is to hook some primitive-style Christmas stockings. They can be a wonderful addition to your fireside décor, or a marvelous gift for someone special.

This stocking design is simple and charming and, like all other rug hooking projects, will take on the character of the wool you select. We chose hand-dyed wool in a mix of plaids, herringbones, checks, and tweeds that add a rich color palette as well as unique texture. The design was hooked with a #8-cut ($1/4$") strip, which really speeds up the hooking time. Color planning is simplified by the use of traditional Christmas colors—reds, greens, and golds. (While several stockings are shown here, the directions that follow focus on the *Argyle Stocking* with the word "Peace" on it.)

Color Planning and Dyeing

Because our preference is a primitive style, we seldom use just one piece of wool for any one area of interest. The

Material used in the hooking of the Argyle Stocking *shown on page 33.*

backgrounds we like are usually composed of at least three different pieces of wool dyed in the same recipe. Even the single line in the *Argyle Stocking* is accomplished with four assorted light pieces of wool thrown into the same dye bath. This is an excellent means of using up small leftover pieces of wool from other projects. When color planning your pattern, plan the background first so that your design can be seen effectively on it. In the argyle pattern, the green is the background; the gold diagonal lines and red squares are the design.

For those of you who love the primitive style, we highly recommend Barbara Carroll and Emma Lou Lais's dye book *Antique Colours for Primitive Rugs* (W. Cushing & Company, Kennebunkport, Maine, 1996) for its dye formulas. We have, however, taken liberty with some of the recipes to produce the reds, greens, and golds we wanted for our *Argyle Stocking*. Use Emma Lou's Favorite Red #12 formula, but substitute Cushing's Egyptian Red dye for Terra Cotta and pour the whole cup of dye solution in the dye

pot. With Emma Lou's Hunter Green #32, mix 1/2 teaspoon each of Hunter Green and Olive Green dyes in the same cup and use the whole cup in the dye bath. Barb's Great Gold #43 works well for the gold, but use just $3/4$ cup of the recipe in the dye bath.

Your results will differ depending on what color you choose for the base wool. We like to mix three different values—light, medium, and dark—in the dye pot to get wonderful variations of the same color. We always try to use a piece of green in the red dye pot, a red in the green dye pot, and beige, tan, or light browns in the gold pot. Depending on how much wool is available, we prefer to put at least four pieces of wool in each dye pot, and sometimes as many as eight small pieces.

Hooking the *Argyle Stocking*

Enlarge the pattern on page 34 and transfer it to the backing of your choice. Our *Argyle Stocking* is approximately 11" x 19". We recommend

An assortment of Jeanne and Pat's other holiday stockings, hooked and finished in the same manner as their Argyle Stocking.

linen or monk's cloth as an easy to use, yet durable backing for primitive designs.

The *Argyle Stocking* was hooked with gold, red, and green wool in a variety of textures. An easy way to mix those textures is to cut your strips in varying lengths and combine them in small plastic bags, one bag for each color. Do not cut your strips too long (12" x 16" maximum) or too short (4" minimum). If you are uncertain about which strip to use next, shut your eyes and dig into the bag containing the appropriate color. The effect of mixing the textures will be a wonderful primitive look.

We encourage our students to have fun with their projects, whether

they're hooking a purple lamb or a green moose. The childlike innocence of the designs and the easy color palette makes primitive hooking a relaxing pastime. While primitive hooking has tremendous flexibility, nothing should detract from the quality of your work. Strive for each loop to be of uniform height. When hooking with a #8-cut strip of wool, your loops should be 1/4" high. The loops should be resting comfortably next to each other, not pushing the loop next to it.

Begin by hooking a border row following the outside line of the stocking, using a variety of green strips. The green line around the edge frames the design area and keeps the

interior colors from appearing as though they are running off the side of the stocking. It will also keep the tails (the ends of the strips) from falling off the edge of the stocking.

Next, hook the gold diagonal lines, remembering to mix your values and textures as you did with the greens. **Do not hook the interior gold line around the red diamond at this time.** You will steadily work your way into the red center diamonds. Now put in the green background, hooking two rows next to the gold diagonal lines. Hook one row of gold against the inside of the green. Finish off the remaining space (it should be a diamond shape) with a mixture of red wools. The last step is to hook the letters and fill in the header space with the green background material.

Blocking

When your hooking is complete, go over your project with one last critical eye, checking for high and low loops. Adjust them as needed. Next, block your stocking.

Place a fluffy towel on an ironing board and put your stocking face down on top of it. Turn the setting on your iron to dry/wool. Liberally dampen a thin tea towel, leaving it quite damp, but not dripping wet. Cover the back of the hooking with the damp towel. Rest your iron for several seconds on the tea towel, then lift it up and lightly steam-press the next part of the stocking until the entire stocking has been pressed. Never exert pressure on your

Argyle Stocking, *11" x 19", #8-cut wool on linen. Designed and hooked by Pat Brooks, Nashville, Tennessee, 2001.*

work when pressing. If necessary, re-wet the tea towel. Turn your work over and repeat the process on the front of the stocking. Allow the stocking to dry by keeping it perfectly flat for approximately 12 hours, depending on your climate.

Assembling the Stocking

With your sewing machine sew a zigzag stitch $1/2$" around the entire stocking. This prevents the foundation from unraveling when it's trimmed. Trim the foundation close

to the zigzag stitching, being careful not to clip the stitches.

1. Use the front of the stocking as your guide to cut a back for it from wool. When cutting the wool for the stocking's back, lay the right side of the stocking down on the right side of the wool backing. Also cut two lining pieces from the cotton fabric. Cut on the straight of the grain and include an extra $1/2$" around the stocking shape.

2. Sew the right side of the hooked stocking to the right side of the

wool backing; sew by hand with a backstitch, using upholstery thread. Be careful not to sew hooked loops into the seam. Sew as closely as possible to the hooked area so that the foundation does not show through.

3. Turn the stocking right-side out. There is no need to trim these seams since the wool has a natural give to it.

4. Press the right and back sides with a dry iron and a damp cloth, being careful to retain a nice stocking shape Allow the stocking to dry flat overnight.

5. Pin the two lining pieces with the right sides together. With cotton thread sew a 1/2" seam allowance. Sew along the sides and heel of the lining, leaving an 8" opening in the toe. Clip the curves, but not their stitching. Turn the lining pieces right-side out and press. Then turn the lining inside out.

6. Insert the hooked stocking into the lining with the right sides together, matching the seams. Using upholstery thread, backstitch by hand around the top of the stocking, leaving a small space next to the back seam to place a loop so the stocking can be hung.

7. To make a loop, cut a strip of backing wool 1 1/2" x 6". Fold it in thirds lengthwise (so it is 3/4" wide) and sew it with a zigzag stitch.

8. Insert the loop into the top of the stocking so its folded edge is in the stocking and the raw edges are lined up against the back seam (the heel side). Sew it securely into place.

9. Slip the lining up and over the

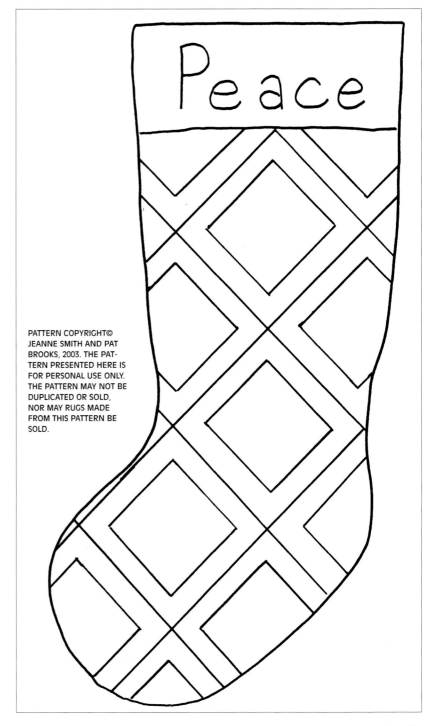

PATTERN COPYRIGHT© JEANNE SMITH AND PAT BROOKS, 2003. THE PATTERN PRESENTED HERE IS FOR PERSONAL USE ONLY. THE PATTERN MAY NOT BE DUPLICATED OR SOLD, NOR MAY RUGS MADE FROM THIS PATTERN BE SOLD.

stocking. The loop should now be visible. Press the lining and turn the seam allowance in at the toe. Slipstitch the toe by hand or topstitch it by machine. To reinforce the loop, topstitch it by machine 1/8" from top of stocking across the back of the stocking.

Jeanne Smith and Pat Brooks are the owners of Primitive Woolens. The Argyle Stocking pattern and others can be ordered by mail. Write to PO Box 25182, Plano, TX 75025-1282 or visit their Web site at www.primitivewoolens.com.

by Barbara Brown

Dog and Bird

With a lesson on hooking with as-is recycled wool

Dog and Bird, *26" x 17", ¹/4" to ³/8" hand-cut wool strips on primitive linen. Designed and hooked by Barbara Brown, Kennebunkport, Maine, 1998.*

When I started hooking many years ago, I lived in the southern United States, and fabric stores did not stock much wool fabric. I haunted thrift shops, buying wool skirts and slacks. Grays and camels were plentiful, but reds and greens were hard to come by. To obtain the colors I needed, I used red, green, and gold dyes over tans and beiges, and blues and purples over grays. Eventually, I ordered wool by mail and was amazed at the variety of reasonably priced fabrics available.

As I began hooking with as-is wool, I noticed it had a liveliness dyed wool did not have. The brightly colored threads in tweeds, plaids, and checks were not dulled by overdyeing. Instead, their brightness was diluted by the duller threads around them.

Now I hook exclusively with as-is wool. Many of my students and other hookers I talk to like the idea of using as-is wool but are unsure of which fabrics to buy. Here are some suggestions.

Choosing Wool

When selecting wool, remember that over a 100-year lifetime, dark colors fade and light or bright colors fade and become soiled. If you want your rug to look 100 years old today, hook it with faded and dirty (dull) versions of the colors used long ago.

Use light and dark neutral (oat-

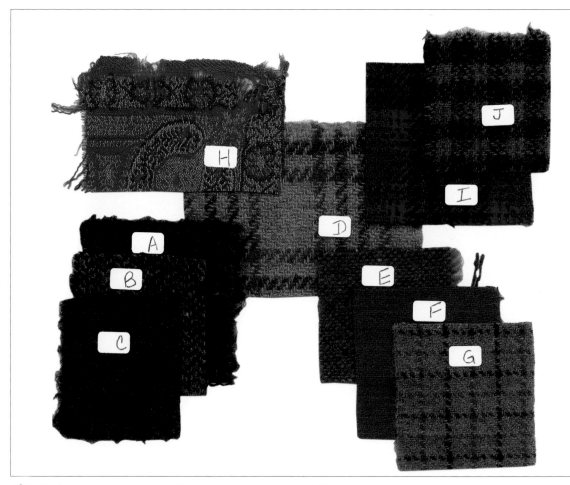

Figure 1: *Samples of the fabrics Barbara Brown used to hook* Dog and Bird.

> *As I began hooking with as-is wool, I noticed it had a liveliness dyed wool did not have. The brightly colored threads in tweeds, plaids, and checks were not dulled by overdyeing.*

meal and charcoal gray-brown) tweeds, checks, heathers, and other textures for backgrounds. Textured fabrics duplicate as nearly as possible loops that over time have become faded, soiled, and worn on top. Buy 1-yard pieces if you like mixed fabric backgrounds; otherwise purchase 1 1/2-yard or 2-yard pieces. This should be enough wool for most medium-size rugs.

When choosing colors, think dirty, tea-dyed, or khaki-drab overdyed. This applies to light neutrals (oatmeal) and all colors. Tweeds, checks, and plaids are good candidates because they are a combination of colorful and neutral or contrasting threads. Accumulate a variety of 1/2-yard pieces.

It is easier to color plan a rug if you have some commonly used fabrics on hand. Purchase several neutral background fabrics that can also be used for animals, tree trunks, roofs, borders, and so on, and 1/2-yard pieces of a variety of dirty reds and greens. Buy medium-light (visible on dark backgrounds), medium, and medium-dark (visible on light backgrounds) values.

These are your basic fabrics and are sometimes all you need. If you need additional colors, choosing them will be easier because you will have a substantial start. Some dirty colors can be hard to find, so buy 1/2-yard pieces of dirty golds, plums, and blues when you see fabrics you like.

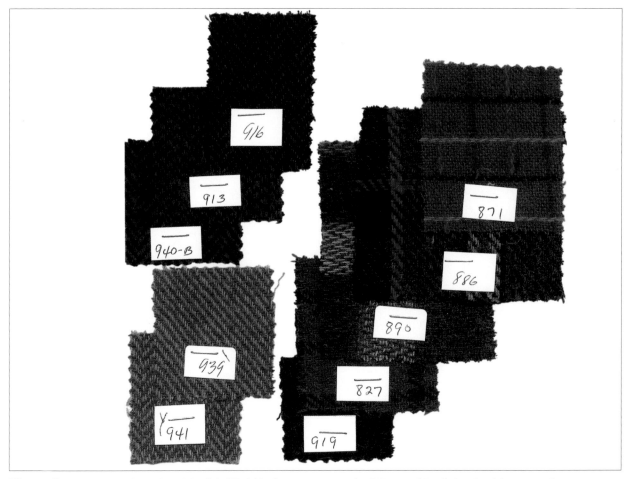

Figure 2: *Samples of fabrics from Mandy's Wool Shed you can use to hook* Dog and Bird. *Similar fabrics may be substituted.*

There is a lot of contrast in texture and pattern between hooked solid fabrics and nonsolids. Take advantage of this to add interest and dimension to your rugs and to differentiate between objects.

Planning Colors for a Primitive Rug

Primitive animal rugs can be simple to color plan. Beginners should choose a small rug, about 3 square feet in area. For this article, I have selected *Dog and Bird* (Port Primitives pattern #213). Enlarge the pattern to 26" x 17". Cover it with a piece of veiling and trace the design with a chisel-point permanent marker.

FABRIC REQUIREMENTS

• **Dog and two rows of border:** 92" x 17" (buy 1 yard)
• **Leaves, grass, and corners:** 35" x 17" (buy 1/2 yard*)
• **Bird, flower, and border:** 31" x 17" (buy 1/2 yard)
• **Pot, bird's beak, and legs:** 4" x 17" (buy 1/2 yard)
• **Background:** 33" X 17" (buy 1/2 yard)
(Minimum purchase is usually 1/2 yard)

Select a piece of backing (Angus burlap, primitive linen, monk's cloth, or rug warp) the size of the rug plus 3" on all sides. Draw a 26" x 17" rectangle in the center of the backing with the marker. Place the veiling pattern in the center of the rectangle and retrace the pattern with the marker so it transfers onto the backing.

Let's plan this rug's colors using our basic neutral, red, and green fabrics. The dog can be hooked in a dark neutral wool on a light neutral background with a bright and dark striped border.

In my rug the dog is dark. I used fabrics A, B, and C in Figure 1 on page 36. You might choose a dark, neutral tweed like Mandy's Wool Shed 916, 913, or 940-B (see Figure 2 above). My light background was fabric D. You can use 939 or 941, two great light neutrals. I used fabrics E, F, and G for the leaves, grass, and corners. You can use an olive-green plaid like 871, 886, 890, or 827 alone or

38

combined with a solid like 919. (See the "Sources" section on page 63 for complete ordering information for Mandy's Wool Shed.) Choose a solid that is distinct from the texture but coordinates well with it. For my flower I used a piece of red paisley (H) and plaids for the bluebird (I and J). You could use red tweed for both the flower and the bird.

So far we have used only basic fabrics. Let's add a chestnut-brown solid for the pot, the bird's beak, and the bird's legs. Primitive borders are usually dark, or bright on the inside edge and dark on the outside if the background is dark. I used charcoal (C) and a blue plaid (J). You may use the dog color (charcoal) and a red tweed. The flower center can be the leaf color, and the animal's eyes the background wool. Feel free to substitute fabrics you have on hand or fabrics from other suppliers.

To prepare your fabrics, wash them in the washer with a little detergent and dry them in the dryer. Tear them as needed into swatches about 3" x 18". Tear parallel to the selvage edge. Cut 1/4"- to 3/8"-wide strips by hand as needed.

Attaching Rug Tape

Now that you are committed to your color plan, attach the rug tape. I bind all my rugs with tape only. Early curtains, bed hangings, and quilts had bound edges, so I figure tape is an authentic finish; my rugs have held up well to 12 years of hard use. On the other hand, many people strongly advocate whipping the edges.

If you decide to use tape, it

If you want your rug to look 100 years old today, hook it with faded and dirty (dull) versions of the colors used long ago.

should match the darkest color in the rug, usually black or dark brown for primitive rugs. Pin it along the outside edge of the pattern with the tape edge inside the line of the pattern. Start on the left side, 4" or 5" from the bottom. Continue pinning the tape around the edge and overlap the ends. Fold the beginning end back on itself, so the cut end is between the overlapped ends. Stitch the tape close to the edge by hand or machine. Add a zigzag stitch 3/4" outside the sewn edge of the tape. Do not cut off the excess backing at this point because you will need it to attach the pattern to your frame.

How to Hook *Dog and Bird*

Once your tape is sewn on the edge, you are ready to hook. Outline and fill each element, beginning with the dog. Hook his body first. Then outline his head, hook the eye with background fabric, encircle it with a row of the dog fabric, and then fill in the rest of the head.

Hook the outer border close to the rug tape and then the inner border row. Fill in the space between the two rows. Then hook

the pot, bird, stem, leaves, and flower, outlining and filling. Next, hook a row of background along the border and around each element. Fill in the rest of the background by following the contours of the elements until you reach the border.

Finishing and Adding Tongues

Press your rug by placing the rug face down on a flat surface and placing a moist (but not sopping wet) towel over it. Then, stamp-press the rug (do not rub it as if ironing clothing) until the entire rug has been pressed. Fold the corners of the excess foundation to the back diagonally and press. With the right side up, press the excess foundation fabric to the back, leaving about two foundation threads showing next to the binding. Trim just outside the zigzag stitch. Turn the tape to the back, covering the raw foundation edge, and slip stitch it in place.

The original of this antique rug had a fabric tongue border, so I put one on mine, too. To make your own, cut two 1/2" x 3 1/4" tongues out of washed and dried coat-weight black wool. Pin them to the back of the rug, blanket stitch the rounded edges with blue-gray thread, and whip the straight edges to the back of the rug. Keep the straight edges even with the hemmed edge of the tape.

The pattern for Dog and Bird *is available printed on premium primitive linen from Barbara Brown's company, Port Primitives, 987 Back Road, Shapleigh, Maine 04076, (207) 490–6933.*

Grandma's Rug

With a lesson on setting color in recycled wool

In 1926, my mother, Anne Jeter, and my grandmother, Florence Dean, took a train across the continent from Medford, Oregon, to eastern Canada. In Nova Scotia, Grandma savored her first taste of rug hooking when they encountered matmakers along the sides of the roads. She was so taken by the technique that upon returning home, she had my grandfather fashion a hook for her from a file and a small block of wood. Grandma taught herself and her mother to hook: as a result of that trip on the Canadian Pacific Railway, five generations of avid rug hookers were born.

As most rug hookers of that era, Grandma was a recycler. She hand-cut half-inch strips of wool and other fabrics from mill ends, family cast-offs, and clothing from church rummage sales. Some of her patterns were purchased at a local department store, as was probably the original rug on which I based this beginner project. *Grandma's Rug* is an adaptation of the center of her rug shown on the right.

For a good-size rug at 38" x 28", *Grandma's Rug* hooks up quickly. (I finished it in three weeks.) As a "hit or miss" rug, it is a colorful project for using your supply of scrap wool and an appropriate first rug for those learning the secrets of recycling. ("Hit or miss" simply refers to using leftover fabrics to hook a rug.) The combination of textures and colors gives the rug a stunning glow without complex hooking and dyeing techniques.

EXCLUSIVE DESIGN: *See the "Exclusive Designs" section after page 32 for a large pull-out pattern of this rug!*

Materials

To hook *Grandma's Rug* as a scrap project or using recycled wool, collect as many as 20 different textured and solid materials: plaids, checks, tweeds, and heathers. If you recycle used clothing, use fabric that is at least 80 percent wool. I prefer pants, bathrobes, and pleated skirts because they disassemble easily and yield the most yardage. Always clean used clothing before using it for hooked rugs.

After washing, tear the wool lengthwise on the warp threads into manageable strips about six inches wide. Cut the strips into 3/8" strips for hooking. You can even use the strips with raw edges; they will not show when packed into the rug. Save small leftover pieces for filling in squares where you run out of material. In "hit or miss" rugs like *Grandma's Rug*, when you run out of one color, finish an element with a fabric of a similar color, value, and texture.

Untitled, *40" x 38", hand-cut wool on burlap. Designer unknown. Hooked by Florence Dean, Medford, Oregon, circa 1920s.*

You will need a total of between 2 1/2 and three pounds of wool for *Grandma's Rug*. For my color plan, I used 3/4 yard of black (middle border and the outlines for the square) and 1/8 yard each of blue, charcoal, beige, and plaid for the other borders. You will need varying amounts of other fabrics for the "hit or miss" squares, depending on the number of textures you use. As an approximate figure, you will use about 18 square inches of fabric for the inside of each square and about nine square inches more for the outline.

Setting Color

Some recycled wool is not wash-fast, so color might bleed from your rug when it gets wet. This is especially true with dark colors: reds, blues, purples, and black. To test for wash-fastness, place a small piece of fabric in a glass of tepid water with a drop of dishwashing liquid. If color bleeds from the fabric, you need to set the color before using the material for hooking. Simply simmer the fabric in two gallons of water with 1/8 cup of vinegar for 50 minutes. When the color is set, the water should be clear. If not, repeat with fresh water and vinegar. (Depending on the amount of fabric and how much color bleeds, you may need to adjust the amount of water and vinegar and the cooking time.) Rinse the wool three times to remove the vinegar, and dry completely before cutting and hooking.

Color Planning

To color plan *Grandma's Rug*, select colors for the flowers first, then plan the rest of the rug to complement them. I used three eight-value swatches: blue, pink and lavender. (A swatch is eight values, or equidistant shades from light to dark, of the same color dyed on separate pieces of wool.) To balance the rug top and bottom, I used four values of a color on a top flower and the other four values of the same color on a bottom flower. For the leaves, I used a variety of leftovers, including blue-greens, basic greens, and spot-dyed greens. If your greens are too unrelated, consider marrying them (placing them all in the dye pot together).

After selecting colors for the flowers, gather a variety of colors and textures for the squares. Begin by finding three or four textures similar to the color of each flower and the leaves; those fabrics will help relate the flowers to the rest of the rug. Then find 10 or 12 complementary fabrics in neutral colors for the rest of the squares and the borders. After gathering all materials, arrange them in front of you, checking to make sure you have a combination of bright/dull and light/dark fabrics for your "hit or miss" rug.

Directions for Hooking

Transfer the design to the backing of your choice (see transferring instructions on page 8). To follow these instructions using the same amounts of wool, enlarge the pattern to 38" x 28". Hook each element in the following order, referring to the photograph on page 42 to see my work loop by loop.

If you use 3/8" strips as I did, you will need to skip more holes than you normally do, even if you are a primitive hooker. Be sure to pull the loops as high as the strip is wide, creating a higher pile for your rug than you may be used to. Because the strips are so wide, pulling the loops up flat is a bit tricky; they tend to fold over. Try pulling the loop up high to unfold it, then pulling it back down to the correct height with your bottom hand. If you are not a perfectionist, leave the loops folded.

Hook the flowers first using four values of each color, starting with the centers. Then, hook the outlines and fill toward the center. (Be sure to stay in the lines of the patterns at all times, so the flowers do not become too large.) Hook the flower values in any order, using the remaining four values for a flower on the opposite side of the rug. Next, hook the leaves with a variety of green fabrics. Because this is an old-fashioned "hit or miss" rug, do not strive for realism with the leaves and flowers. Maintain a primitive look.

Using black wool, hook the innermost border and grid between the squares. As you move around the rug, carefully remove it from the frame or hoop, so the grids do not pull out. After the grid is hooked, work on the squares, outlining each with textured material and filling with another. Hook from the center outward.

When hooking the squares, use a variety of solid and textured materials. To achieve a balanced "hit or miss" look for the rug, concentrate on

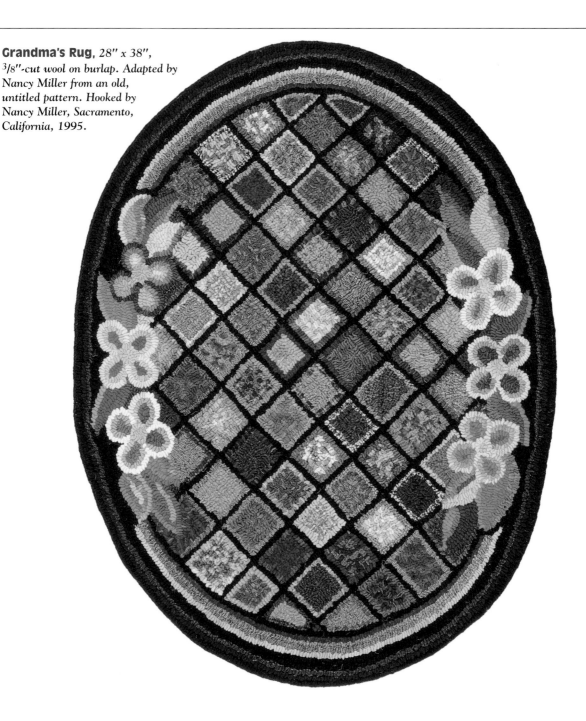

Grandma's Rug, *28″ x 38″,*
3/8″-cut wool on burlap. Adapted by
Nancy Miller from an old,
untitled pattern. Hooked by
Nancy Miller, Sacramento,
California, 1995.

spreading all textures, colors, and values uniformly across the rug. For example, do not pull all the blue fabrics on one side of the rug, or it will look unbalanced.

After completing the inside of the rug, hook the borders last. Ideally, use dark values of materials that are repeated in the interior of the rug.

Finishing

Refer to the basic finishing instructions on page 9 before you begin hooking *Grandma's Rug*. Proper finishing techniques are time-consuming and can be difficult to master, so consult a teacher if possible. Never skimp on finishing the edges. Otherwise, your rug may not live on

for generations of enjoyment, as does my grandmother's original rug.

A fourth-generation rug hooker, Nancy Miller owns Miller Rug Hooking, 2448 Brentwood Road, Sacramento, California 95825, (916) 482–1234. She sells complete kits for Grandma's Rug. Jane McGown Flynn has a similar pattern available through House of Price.

by Mary Ann Goetz

Patriotic Heart

With a lesson on mottling wool

I designed *Patriotic Heart* a few years ago for a beginner's class I was to teach just before Independence Day. I thought it would be fun to do an appropriate piece for the holiday. I've always loved anything that incorporates the red, white, and blue colors of the flag. I think it has to do with my military background, as I was brought up in a military family and went into the Army myself out of college. I was an Army nurse during Vietnam and retired after Desert Storm. I have a large hooked wall-hanging that I completed during Desert Storm (spent in Fort Hood, Texas) that will forever hold special memories for me.

We Texans have a special affinity for our state flag. It's found in a lot of crafts and other decorative pieces. I designed a "Remember The Alamo" piece that had the slogan placed around the Texas state flag. It has been a popular pattern for pillows. I felt hooking something with a variation on our national flag was a good step to take next.

I am also crazy about hearts. I have more hooked hearts on wall-hangings, pillows, and rugs than any other motif. My home has heart wreaths, heart ceramics, and even a wooden heart clock. You can see, then, that my *Patriotic Heart* design perfectly incorporates three of my loves: hearts, my nation's flag, and primitive hooking.

Patriotic Heart, *8" x 20", #8-cut wool on linen. Designed and hooked by Mary Ann Goetz, Spring, Texas, 1999.*

The Design and Materials

While I found this pattern appealing, it had to be practical as well. It had to meet my criteria for a beginner's project—to be not too detailed, too big, or have too many curving lines.

Patriotic Heart is a simple wall-hanging with a lot of straight lines in it. Beginners need to hook straight lines to get a rhythm going to pull up their loops to the same height. They also need the confidence gained by finishing their first piece in a reasonably short amount of time. They will never get "hooked" on the craft if their first project is too big and complicated, and this design's size (8" x 20") is just right for them.

Once the design was decided upon, I selected my tools and materials for the project. I think the rug hooking frame is the most important tool for this craft after the hook. Hooking is more enjoyable when your backing is nice and taut, and that requires a good frame. I always have my beginner students use a quilting hoop. Linen (my foundation of choice because its holes are well defined) stays taut on a hoop better than burlap or monk's cloth.

For this wallhanging, I recommend using light gray wool for the red stripes, white or natural wool for the white strips, navy and light gray for the top of the heart, and a navy tweed or herringbone for the background. Some of this wool I dyed using the formulas noted on this page. I rip the wool into ¹/₂ yard pieces (18" x 60") then divide that into six pieces that are 18" x 10" each. Each 18" x 10" piece yields around 30 strips in a #8 cut. For the three red stripes on the flag, you'll need 40 strips: for the four white stripes, 40 strips. For the blue curved portions of the heart, you'll need 30 strips. The background will require four 18" x 10" pieces.

Dyeing Formulas and Methods

I didn't want bright red and white colors in this primitive project, so I dyed my colors using PRO Chem brand dyes for a darker, more mottled effect. Here's my formula for the red used in the flag:

- ¹/₄ tsp #550 chestnut
- ¹/₂ tsp #351 bright red

Mix the dyes in 1 cup of boiling water. Pour the entire mixture into a large dye pot of 1¹/₂ gallons of boiling water. Add four to six glugs of white vinegar to change the acidity of the water and thus enhance the performance of the dyes. (Since vinegar is the mordant that makes the wool pick up the dye, you can add more of it later if the dye bath isn't clearing.) Put into the dye bath six pieces of 18" x 10" light gray wool that has been soaked in Synthrapol or Wetter Than Wet (wetting agents that help the fabric absorb dye).

You want the wool to be mottled with the formula's color, not uniformly dyed, so scrunch it into the pot and only stir it enough to get it all below the water line. Let it simmer for 20 minutes, and stir it lightly again. Let the wool simmer until the dye bath is clear. Remember that the less stirring you do to the wool, the more mottling you'll have. Rinse the wool in cold water water to remove the vinegar.

I wanted the white stripes to be mottled as well. Here's the formula I used for them:

- ¹/₈ tsp #550 chestnut in 1 cup of boiling water.

Stir the dye powder into 1 cup of boiling water. Scrunch two 18" x 10" pieces of white or natural wool in a pot with 1 quart of boiling water and some vinegar. (You'll use less water than before because you have less wool to dye.) The wool should have soaked in Synthrapol or Wetter Than Wet prior to dyeing. Add small drops of the chestnut dye mixture to the pot, as it's very easy to get the wool too dirty looking—you don't want brown stripes. Simmer the wool for 20 minutes. When you have the color you want, rinse the wool in cold water.

I used both solid navy wool and dyed mottled blue for the top of the heart. For the mottled blue I came up with this formula:

- ¹/₂ tsp #413 navy
- ¹/₈ tsp #672 black
- ¹/₈ tsp #490 blue

Use the same technique here that you used to dye the red in the flag. In this case, you'll be dyeing two pieces of light gray wool. If the wool ends up being too dark for

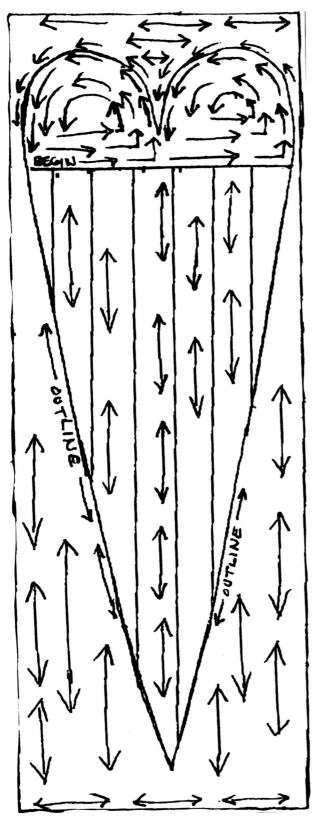

BEGIN

OUTLINE

OUTLINE

OUTLINE

your taste, use little or no black the next time.

Any navy tweed or herringbone looks good as a contrasting background. (I used a navy and white herringbone in mine.) The blue humps at the top of the heart must not be too similar in color to the blue background, or you'll lose the definition of the heart shape. This pattern requires four pieces of 18" x 10" wool for the background. A border could be added using two or three rows of the red or white, but I decided to keep it simple for the beginner.

Before I move on to the hooking instructions for *Patriotic Heart*, let me comment on the dye pans I used—and on another way to dye. I have found several inexpensive, white enamel instrument pans at antique stores. They were used to sterilize surgical instruments before autoclaves were invented. They are great for simmering and dyeing small amounts of wool. These pans typically measure about 8" x 6" x 4" deep. I can place a piece of wool almost flat in it, and then I can drip my dye randomly onto the wool as it soaks in $1/2$" of boiling water with a little vinegar added. Then, I can turn the wool over and drip the dye on the other side. This is another technique for mottling wool.

How to Hook
Patriotic Heart
Begin hooking this pattern by outlining both humps of the heart shape. These humps are the only

areas of the piece that do not contain straight lines, so they will be the most difficult area to hook if you are a beginner. Then simply fill in the humps by hooking U-shaped rows, one after the other, against the outline row until the humps are filled in completely.

If you prefer to practice on straight lines first and do the curved humps later, hook the center red stripe, placing four rows of #8-cut wool in the stripe. If you use a

ground material. You will now see the heart shape defined by that single background row outlining it. Put in another curved row of hooking over the blue humps at the top of the piece.

Then hook straight horizontal rows to fill in the top of the background. Hook vertical rows down each side. It is important to have the same number of rows on each side of the heart to have the design centered. Stay in the same row of

the finished effect will be much smoother.

Finishing Up

Patriotic Heart is meant to be a wall-hanging, so it is finished differently and more easily than a rug. Steam the piece on a flat surface with a steam iron or under a wet cloth. Steam both sides. I machine sew cotton binding tape right up next to the edge of the hooking on all four sides. Trim the linen backing, so it is covered by the width of the cotton binding tape and is not visible when the tape is turned under. Turn the tape under, fold the corners, pin it, and steam it down. Whipstitch the tape all the way around the edge. At the top of the wallhanging, stitch onto the tape two loops of 2" cotton binding tape. These loops can support a 6" length of wooden dowel. Using this, you can hang your lovely piece right on the wall of your choice.

The finishing touch for my piece is sewing three old buttons at the top of the flag's red stripes. I love old buttons on hooking projects. One of my students put ceramic stars on her flag instead of buttons, which also looked very cute (they can be attached with a glue gun). Once you are satisfied with this easy project, hang it, and salute your new flag!

I've always loved anything that incorporates the red, white, and blue colors of the flag. I am also crazy about hearts. My Patriotic Heart design perfectly incorporates three of my loves: hearts, my nation's flag, and primitive hooking.

smaller cut of wool, put in five or six rows.

The stripes are hooked with allowances for four rows of #8-cut wool strips per stripe. The center stripe is red, which gives you three red and four white stripes. The white stripes on the outer edge may not match perfectly in the number or rows they contain, but perfection is not what we're all about in primitive hooking. End each row at the pattern line drawn on the linen. Don't cross the lines, as it may cause your design to get too large.

The background contains almost double the amount of hooked loops as the heart. Begin it by outlining the entire heart with your back-

holes on the linen background, and your hooked rows will remain straight. Also be sure to hook one or two horizontal rows at the very bottom of the piece. Otherwise, tail ends of the vertical strips will hang off the end of each row of your finished piece at the edge. A horizontal row helps tuck in the tails.

Vary the length of your strips as you hook straight consecutive lines. Your wool strips will be cut all the same length (roughly 18 inches), and thus they will all end at the same point if you do not vary their length. That ending point will have an obvious line or dent. Avoid that by varying your strip lengths. You may waste a few inches of wool, but

Patriotic Heart is available as a pattern or kit from Mary Ann Goetz, 10623 Cherrybrook Circle, Highlands Ranch, CO 80126, (330) 683–3330.

by Pat Brooks and Jeanne Smith

Primitive Lamb

With a lesson on binding round rugs

Primitive Lamb I, *25" x 21", #8-cut wool on linen. Designed by Primitive Woolens. Hooked by Jeanne Smith, McKinney, Texas, 1999.*

Our love of old, primitive hand-crafted rugs led us down the wonderful path of rug hooking. We admire the charm and childlike innocence of some early examples and have reproduced that effect in *Primitive Lamb*, which we've hooked in two versions. Through the use of color and technique, it is possible to achieve the same innocence and charm in your rugs.

Muted colors play a vital role in the overall effect of a primitive rug. In authentic primitive rugs, time has done the work of giving wool an aged look. You need to achieve that look in your new rugs through your dye pot.

One way to successfully reduce the color intensity of your wool is to stew it. Place several pieces of wool from the same color family in a pot of water, and stew them together for at least an hour. The colors will meld and, when combined in hooking, will result in a mottled or scrappy look and an overall aged effect. The colors retain their own character but are more pleasing to the eye. Add a piece of light tan or white to the stew pot to get a very

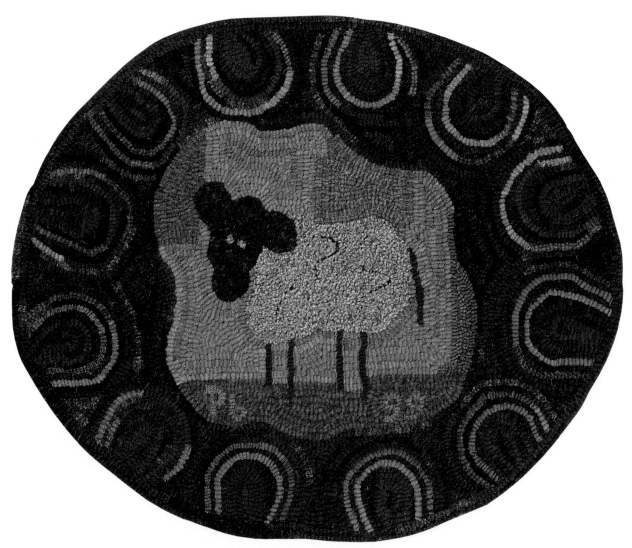

Primitive Lamb II, *25" x 21", #8-cut wool on linen. Designed by Primitive Woolens. Hooked by Pat Brooks, Gallitin, Tennessee, 1999.*

light version of the color. Another way to tone down hues is to overdye wool with Cushing's Khaki Drab or Bright Purple dyes.

Hooking Tips

When hooking innocent primitives, keep in mind that realism is not your goal. The sky does not have to be blue; the grass does not have to be green; and traditional trees are out. There is no shading to worry about, no precise lines, and few color mistakes.

A few guidelines, however, will help you achieve the primitive look you're after. Use plaids, tweeds, and checks to add rich texture and character to your projects. When purchasing wool, scrunch each piece into little accordion pleats with your fingers, so you will get an accurate idea of what it will look like hooked. Basic colors you should always look for are beiges, browns, reds, greens, blues, and golds.

We use #8-cut strips and pull our loops up to approximately ¼" in height. If your wool is wider than a #8,

the height of your loops should match the width of your strips. Some of our students prefer to cut their wool by hand; the uneven widths add another primitive element to their work. Regardless of how you cut your strips, always cut the wool with the grain of the fabric.

We use premium linen as the foundation for our rugs. It may cost a little more, but it is less fibrous than burlap and will endure the test of time.

When you hook a primitive, outline and fill each detail in the interior

of the design; then hook two straight rows of the background color against the border to prevent distortion along the edge. Start the border by hooking a straight line around the entire pattern close to the binding edge. Then fill in the rest of the border between that outline row and the rows of background wool.

Attaching one edge of the binding to the linen beyond the border line prior to hooking makes the finishing process easier. This also makes it less likely that you will have gaps between the body of your work and the binding edge. The binding may be attached by machine or by hand. (See the sidebar on page 51 for instructions on attaching binding tape to a round or oval rug.) At the same time, add a zigzag stitch to the backing about 1/2" beyond where the binding is attached to it. Do not cut away the excess backing until the project is hooked.

Color Planning

To hook our *Primitive Lamb*, begin by planning colors in the two backgrounds of the rug—the one behind the lamb and the one in the border. The objective is to strive for enough contrast to allow each element to be identifiable. High contrast is not necessary in primitive hooking.

For the next step, gather your courage and select a color for the lamb. Be brave—go for a green lamb, or perhaps try purple, as Jeanne did. (If you are using the same color for his face and body, you'll want to outline his face with a contrasting color to allow it to show against his body.)

Overdyed wools from Primitive Lamb I for the lamb's tongues (top and second rows), the center background (third row), and the lamb and the border background (bottom row).

How to Hook *Primitive Lamb*

Before beginning to hook this pattern, read the transferring, hooking, and finishing instructions that begin on page 8. Enlarge the pattern on page 49 to 25" x 21", and transfer it to linen or the backing of your choice.

Start with the lamb's face, first hooking a few loops of the center's background color for the eyes. Hook the head by following its contours. (The purple version also has some of the body color pulled into the head as

The borders of both rugs were hooked with scraps. If you do not possess a stash of wool, select one color for the curved lines of the lamb's tongue and another for their centers. If you really want to be adventurous, use three or four different colors for the centers. Picking up one of the colors from the center of the work and repeating it in the border gives continuity to a piece. This can be seen in both our versions of *Primitive Lamb*.

COLOR PLANS FOR *PRIMITIVE LAMB*

All of the formulas we used for our two lamb rugs, which are noted below, are from *Antique Colours for Primitive Rugs* by Barbara Carroll and Emma Lou Lais (W. Cushing & Co., 1997) using Cushing's Acid Dyes. We have also included the amount of wool required for each section.

PRIMITIVE LAMB I

This version of our pattern is predominantly purple and green, with scraps of rusty red, black, and gold. The scrappy look was created by randomly selecting varying lengths of the green and purple. The lamb's tongues surrounding the central design pulled in the other hues, along with colors from the lamb and backgrounds.
- **Lamb (3" x 12") and border background ($^3/_4$ yard):** #14 Deep Purple, dyed full strength over assorted grays, a brown tweed, and a wide black-and-red stripe.
- **Center background ($^1/_2$ yard):** #29 Khaki/Bronze, dyed full strength over camel, a camel-and-red check, and a beige tweed.
- **Lamb's face, legs, and tail (scraps):** #88 Hook Book Black, dyed full strength over dark grays and a wide black-and-red stripe.
- **Lamb's tongues (scraps):** #43 Barb's Great Gold and #12 Emma Lou's Favorite Red (we substituted Egyptian Red

for the Terra Cotta to get a rustier red) dyed full strength over assorted solids, checks, and tweeds; assorted scraps from the lamb's face and body.

PRIMITIVE LAMB II

The second version of this design has a patchwork background behind the lamb. Five different wools were dyed to achieve the scrappy look in the border background. They were cut to a variety of lengths and randomly drawn out of a bag. Random scraps were used in the lamb's tongues, too. The wool in the lamb's face is also found in the border. The quantities are the same as in *Primitive Lamb I*.
- **Border background and lamb's face ($^3/_4$ yard):** #90 Antique Black, dyed full strength over assorted reds, blues, grays, and browns.
- **Lamb's body (3" x 12"):** as-is gray herringbone.
- **Center background ($^1/_2$ yard):** #34 Saturday Surprise, dyed full strength over plaids and solids.
- **Lamb's tongues (scraps):** #12 Emma Lou's Favorite Red, dyed with $^1/_2$ cup of dye solution over assorted red plaids; #49 Mustard ($^1/_2$ cup) and #25 Bronze/Green (full strength) dyed over assorted plaids, checks, and tweeds; scraps from the background and scrap bag.

Overdyed wools from Primitive Lamb II *for the lamb (top left corner), the center background (rest of top row), the border background (second row), and the lamb's tongues (third and bottom rows).*

accents.) Next, outline the body inside the pattern's line, and fill it in a random way. Then, hook single rows of wool for the tail and legs in a color darker than the lamb's body.

Next hook the center background. Hook a row of background wool around the entire lamb, and a row inside the outer edge of the center. Fill in the center following the lamb's contours, or in a patchwork fashion as in *Primitive Lamb II*.

Divide the background into uneven sections, and use different wool for each to create the notion that you ran out of one piece and had to choose another. Drop strips from three or four different pieces of wool in a basket or bag, and randomly draw out one strip at a time (no peeking) to achieve a scrappy look.

Hook a row of the border's background around the center background. Then hook two rows around the perimeter of the pattern. Next hook each lamb's tongue, starting in the center and following the arched shape. When all of the lamb's tongues have been hooked, fill in the background around them by hooking around their contours.

Your last step will be to steam-press your rug with a damp cloth and a dry iron. Be careful to not put pressure on your rug; the steam will do the work for you. Steam both sides, and allow

your rug to dry flat for 24 hours. Trim the excess linen up to the zigzag stitch, and fold the binding to the back. Use a whipstitch to attach the edge of the binding tape to the back of the rug. Repeat the steaming process, paying particular attention to the edges.

As you can see, through the use of color and technique it is possible to create your own primitive rug from a

purchased design. We hope you've enjoyed your venture into innocent primitives and are already planning your next project!

Pat Brooks and Jeanne Smith are the proprietors of Primitive Woolens, PO Box 251282, Plano, Texas 75025-1282, www.primitivewoolens. com. They provide the pattern for Primitive Lamb *on linen or in a kit.*

ATTACHING TAPE TO A ROUND OR OVAL RUG

To attach binding tape to a round or oval rug, take a permanent marker with a broad, flat tip, and trace over the pattern's outside border line. This widens the line, giving you a larger mark to place your binding against. Align the outside edge of the binding tape along the outer edge of the widened border line, working from the inside of the design (see the illustration). Pin the tape in place. Stitch the tape around its outside edge with a 1/8" to 1/16" seam allowance. Fold the binding back to hook. This still gives you the original border line to hook on. Hook to within one linen thread of the tape. We use black binding for many of

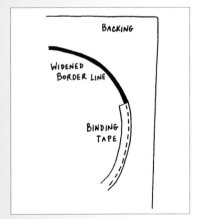

our projects, and the extended black line disguises any area where we did not hook close to the binding.

Pumpkin Moonshine

Rug hookers draw inspiration from many sources: from nature to memories to favorite photographs. Many fiber artists are also inspired by works from other media, especially paintings, both contemporary and historical.

Most of us have one or more favorite artists. Whether you design your own hooked pieces or adapt purchased patterns, think about putting something into your design that reminds you of your favorite artist's work. It will make your hooking experience all the more fun and meaningful.

There are many ways to do this. For example, if Monet is your favorite, you might incorporate the colors and styles of his garden paintings into your work, particularly if your pattern includes water. Think of the lovely, watery blues you could get from a casserole dyeing session. Study the paintings you love and collect, or dye wool with those colors in mind. Let yourself be inspired by your chosen artist's creativity.

My favorite artist has always been Vincent van Gogh. The sky in *Pumpkin Moonshine* was directly inspired by a visit to a traveling exhibit from the van Gogh museum in Amsterdam. Viewing more than 70 paintings in one show was a great opportunity to see recurring themes and color schemes. Van Gogh liked to paint green skies for both night and day, as well as stars in motion (think of his famous painting, *Starry Night*). When I conceived the *Pumpkin*

EXCLUSIVE DESIGN: *See the "Exclusive Designs" section after page 32 for a large pull-out pattern of this rug!*

Moonshine design, I incorporated a green night sky, with motion lines around the stars and a spiraling, crescent moon. I love van Gogh's use of vibrant color and visual motion, which is also an ever-present influence in my work.

Pumpkin Moonshine depicts a pumpkin field on a crisp fall night. There's a magical crescent moon rising, and the stars are popping into view as the sky darkens. You get the feeling that the pumpkin just might turn into Cinderella's coach if given the chance. The night sky is dark, but the pumpkin remains a vivid orange, as if someone were standing nearby with a lantern, ready to carry the pumpkin away. My intent was to create a feeling of expectation when you look at the design. Through the careful use of color and light, you can add mystery to any hooked scene.

Plan Your Colors

The first step in interpreting this pattern is to plan the colors. Let's start with the sky. To follow my color plan, you will need medium and light green, and a darker blue-green. I used Cushing's Myrtle Green dyed over natural wool. Take a piece of wool measuring 3 square feet (12" x 36") and rip off a 12" x 3" strip. To prepare the wool for dyeing, soak it in warm water for 1 hour with a little Ivory soap or a wetting agent like

Synthrapol or Wetter than Wet. Then mix up a dye pot of 1/8 teaspoon of Myrtle Green in 1½ gallons of water with ½ cup of vinegar. Dye the larger piece of wool at a simmer until the water is pale green, then remove the wool to a waiting pot of simmering clear water and ½ cup of vinegar.

You should still have a dye pot of pale Myrtle Green. Add the 12" x 3" strip of wool to the dye pot and let it take up the rest of the dye; simmer it for 30 minutes. Meanwhile, carefully rip a 12" x 12" piece from the large piece of medium-green wool and scrunch it into a 2-quart glass saucepan with a little simmering water and ¼ cup of vinegar. Dissolve 1/16 teaspoon of Royal Blue dye in 2 cups of hot water and spoon the solution onto the scrunched wool in the sauce pan. Your goal is to randomly spot the green wool with the blue dye. Allow all the green wools to steep another 30 minutes before rinsing and drying them.

Now let's prepare the colors for the pumpkin, which will require five oranges and two browns. The oranges range from a deep red-orange to a pale golden-orange. I dyed mine over natural wool with Cushing's Orange, Wine, and Turkey Red dyes, using the following formulas. Simmer the wool until the water clears, and then simmer it an additional 30 minutes to set the color.

Deepest orange: One 4" x 12" piece of wool. 1/16 teaspoon of Turkey

Pumpkin Moonshine, *15" x 15", #4-cut wool on polyester/cotton. Designed and hooked by Patti Patrick, Bloomington, Indiana, 1999.*

Red + 1/16 teaspoon of Orange + 1/16 teaspoon of Wine in 1 1/2 gallons of water with 1/2 cup of vinegar.

Strongest orange: 4" x 12". 1/8 teaspoon of Turkey Red + 1/8 teaspoon of Orange in 1 gallon of water with 1/2 cup of vinegar.

Pale orange: 4" x 12". 1/16 teaspoon of Turkey Red + 1/16 teaspoon of Orange in 1 1/2 gallons of water with 1/2 cup of vinegar.

Golden-orange: 4" x 12". 1/8 teaspoon of Orange in 1 gallon of water with 1/2 cup of vinegar.

Pale gold-orange: 2" x 12". 1/16 teaspoon of Orange in 1 1/2 gallons of water with 1/2 cup of vinegar.

For the field and the pumpkin stem you will need two 2" x 15" pieces of brown wool, one dark and one light. You can pluck from your stash of swatches or dye wool for this project. For dark brown, I recommend 1/4 teaspoon of Cushing's Seal Brown in 1 gallon of water with 1/2 cup of vinegar. For light brown, use 1/16 teaspoon in 1 1/2 gallons of water. The field is a good place to use any plaid or hounds-

tooth wool you've been collecting. For my field's furrows, I overdyed a gray plaid with 1/4 teaspoon of Seal Brown in 1 gallon of water. I kept half of the 10" x 10" wool light in hue and the other half I dip dyed from light to dark.

A 3" x 12" piece of dip-dyed lavender wool is sufficient for the moon and the star motion lines and the moon's spiral. I used 1/4 teaspoon of Cushing's Purple in 1 gallon of water with 1/2 cup of vinegar. While wearing heavy rubber gloves or using tongs, dip the whole piece in the bath quickly. Continue dipping the strip, first halfway up the length and then each time dipping less of the wool until the water clears.

For the moon I used a 3" x 12" piece of wool lightly dyed with Buttercup Yellow. (Use 1/16 teaspoon of dye in 1 1/2 gallons of water with 1/2 cup of vinegar.) The stars are extremely pale pink, green, and blue.

The best choice for the leaf and tendrils is three green wools in light, medium, and dark values. Pull them from your wool supply to dye them using Hunter Green in three strengths. In 1 gallon of water with 1/2 cup of vinegar, dye them using 1/4 teaspoon of dye for dark green, 1/8 teaspoon for medium, and 1/16 teaspoon for light green.

To hook the barn you will need a small amount of wool in red or burgundy, as well as a little black and a light red or pink (See the wool requirements sidebar above) For the border, I used dark purple from a recycled skirt. You could use any dark shade of purple wool you have, or perhaps gray wool dyed with Plum (1/4 teaspoon in 1 gallon of water).

How to Hook
Pumpkin Moonshine

Before you begin hooking this pattern, read the transferring, hooking, and finishing instructions that begin on page 8. Enlarge the pattern in the "Exclusive Designs" section to 15" x 15", and transfer it to the backing of your choice. I advocate using monk's cloth or linen as your backing. Next you'll need to choose the cut or width of your wool strips. I suggest using the middle cut of #5, although you should try a few strands of the narrow #3 cut

WOOL REQUIREMENTS

- **Background:** 432 sq. in. or 12" x 36"
- **Pumpkin:** 216 sq. in. or 12" x 18"
- **Stem:** 30 sq. in. or 2" x 15"
- **Moon and stars:** 72 sq. in. or 6" x 12"
- **Motion lines:** 36 sq. in. or 3" x 12"
- **Leaf and tendrils:** 36 sq. in. or 3" x 12"
- **Field:** 200 sq. in. or 10" x 20"
- **Barn:** 25 sq. in. or 2 1/2" x 10"
- **Border:** 504 sq. in. or 18" x 28"

and the 1/4"-wide #8 cut just for the experience. You will quickly gravitate toward a particular width.

Let's begin with the moon. Using the dark end of the dip-dyed purple wool, start hooking the moon's spiral from its tightest point. Hook the wool right on the pattern line. Use the pale purple to finish outlining the crescent; next, fill in the crescent using the pale yellow wool. Now, starting at the center and following the spiral movement, fill in the background of the moon spiral with the lightest green wool.

After you've finished the moon, hook the pumpkin. With the pale gold-orange, hook the outline of the pumpkin sections as shown in the photo. Next using the golden-orange, follow the contours of the pumpkin to begin hooking the sections. Keep referring to the color photo as you hook inward, using the darker oranges as in my example until the pumpkin is complete.

Follow the color photo for the placement of the light and dark brown wools as you hook the stem. Think of the moon as a light source to determine where the shadows would fall.

Now move to the stars; they are hooked in pale shades of blue, green,

and pink. Hook each star in a different color, first outlining and then filling it. Use the pale purple from the moon's outline to hook the motion lines around the stars.

To hook the barn, use the palest red for the roof lines and a darker red for the sides of the barn. Hook the doorway and the hayloft in black.

Use your two browns to hook the field. Be sure to hook in converging lines to accentuate the furrows and create depth. Alternate the light brown wool and the dip-dyed light-to-dark wool.

Hook the leaf and tendril by first outlining them with the lightest green. Then work inward on the leaf using darker greens. Use the darkest green to hook the front of the leaf.

Now you are ready to fill in the background. Using the medium green wool, start at the center horizon line and hook upward toward the moon and around the pumpkin stem. Keep working upward until you reach the underside of the moon and stars. Keep an eye on the color photo as you fill the background, so you don't move into the area around the stars.

Using the blue-spotted green wool, start filling in around the stars and top of the moon. As you hook around the stars and moon, make sure to circle the motifs with your rows of hooking to create a sense of motion in the sky. See the drawing in the "Exclusive Designs" section for help.

Now you're ready for the border. Use purple wool to fill the space. Be sure to hook two rows parallel to the outer boundary line of the project. This will create a smooth line for finishing the edge.

By Kim Dubay

Sunflower Garden

**With a lesson on
dyeing wool with
coffee and tea**

This pattern of a crow eyeing a garden's delights—a design I created years ago—remains a favorite among primitive hookers. At 36" x 18", it is a nice size for a first rug and can fit into any home. The design offers elements to make the rug interesting to hook, yet needs few colors to make it visually appealing. Crows and sunflowers have yet to become a tiresome combination.

Consider the Background First

As you look at the design, you must first decide how the background should be treated. I chose a neutral background to set off the rich colors of the sunflowers and the brown-black of

EXCLUSIVE DESIGN: See the "Exclusive Designs" section after page 32 for a large pull-out pattern of this rug!

the fence. Some may choose a sky and grass combination with a white picket fence. This step is necessary before any hooking can be done. If you decide to change colors from what I've selected, substitute your choices for those listed in the sidebar on page 57.

Once your decision is made, pick a matching or contrasting color of binding tape to finish the edge. Matching your background color is always best. If you can't find a perfect match at the fabric store, white tape can be dyed. Put the tape into the dye pot when you're dyeing your background wool.

Be sure to add a few extra inches of tape, because it will shrink in the bath. A contrasting color used in the rug can be brought to the edge as an alternative. This rug has two colors touching the border (the background and grass), but I matched the tape to the background because it was the larger area. (For instructions on how to finish your rug with binding tape and whipping, see page 9.)

I always attach my tape first, so I have a straight edge to hook against when I hook my border rows. If you're using burlap, make sure to get primi-

DYEING WOOL WITH COFFEE AND TEA

My sunflower-gold hue was created with Cushing's old union dyes, which are no longer available. Here is a technique for getting a wonderful mustard-yellow without using commercial dyes.

BLEEDING WOOL WITH COFFEE

You will need 1/3 pound of assorted light wools (I used light tan and pale green), 1/4 pound of bleeder wool (I used a bright gold), and 3 1/2 cups of leftover brewed coffee.

Bring to a boil a pot with enough water in it to cover the wool. Add 2 tablespoons of kosher salt, the wool (which has been soaked in hot water with a wetting agent such as Synthrapol or Wetter Than Wet), and the coffee. Simmer the wool with the coffee for 20 minutes or more, depending on how quickly the dye leaves the gold wool. Then add 1/3 cup of white vinegar to the pot, and let it simmer for 20 minutes. Let the wool cool in the pot, and then rinse it in warm water. The tan and green pieces will turn gold, and the coffee will dull them to a soft mustard-yellow.

For my sunflower centers, I used an as-is gold-and-black herringbone. You could use the formula above to dye over a black-and-white herringbone or any black-and-

white tweed to get the same effect.

I suggest keeping samples of each wool for comparison of "before" and "after" colors. Staple them to an index card, and keep a file with all your formulas. Don't forget to write down the amounts of wool used, cooking times, and the amounts of dyes, even if you used coffee or tea.

DYEING BACKGROUNDS WITH TEA

I used tea to dye my tan background. Teas will vary, as will the water in your area, but experiment; you may find a lovely color with your own combination of tea and water.

You will need 1/2 pound of white or natural wool and six tea bags. (Orange pekoe and black pekoe are the blends I use.) Soak the wool in hot water with detergent or a wetting agent. Bring 6 cups of water to a boil and add 2 tablespoons of kosher salt. Add the tea bags and allow them to steep for 5 minutes. After the tea is made, remove the bags, but don't throw them away. Add the wool to the tea and place the tea bags on top of the wool. Simmer everything for 20 minutes and then add 1/3 cup of white vinegar, simmering the wool for an additional 20 minutes. Let the wool cool in the pot; then rinse it well in warm water. Be sure to keep samples of the wool before and after dyeing it and keep a record of all amounts used.

tive burlap, which is large enough to accommodate a #8-cut ($1/4"$) strip. Don't forget to sew a zigzag stitch $1/2"$ beyond your design edge to keep the foundation from fraying once it's cut. After these steps are completed, you are ready to begin hooking.

How to Hook
Sunflower Garden

Read the basic hooking directions on page 8 before beginning. Hook the motifs with the outline-and-fill method. Always start with the center motif—in this case, the crow. Hook

him in black wool. A suggestion I give to hookers who have bought this design is to start the outline at the crow's left toe on his left foot. (To prevent the crow from becoming larger than the drawn image, make sure to hook your outline row inside the drawn line.) Hook around the crow's body until you reach the right toe of the right foot. (See the directional lines on the pattern in the "Exclusive Designs" section.) Begin the second row at the middle toe on his left foot, and end at the middle toe on his right. Do the same for the third outline row.

This works better than trying to outline each foot because his toes become lost that way. For the crow's eye, use a strip of sunflower-bold. Bring up the end of the strip, then one loop in the next hole, and then the tail in the first hole. Cut the strip so you have one loop and two cut tails as your eye. Hook around it with the black wool to hold it in place. Continue to fill in the crow.

Next, hook the fence in a brown-and-black herringbone by outlining each post down to the binding at the bottom and then filling each with ver-

FABRIC REQUIREMENTS

- **Sunflowers:** 6 pieces measuring 6" x 13" each in light tan and pale green dyed gold with coffee (see the dyeing sidebar for the formula)
- **Sunflower centers:** 1 piece measuring 11 1/2" x 16" in a gold-and-black herringbone
- **Fence:** 4 pieces measuring 16" x 16" each in a brown-and-black herringbone
- **Crow:** 1 piece measuring 12" x 17" in jet black
- **Leaves and stems:** 1 piece measuring 17" x 19" in green
- **Grass:** 2 pieces measuring 10" x 13" each in a tan-and-green herringbone
- **Background:** 6 pieces measuring 8" x 13" each in white or natural wool dyed with tea (see the dyeing sidebar)

Sunflower Garden, *36" x 18", #8-cut wool on burlap. Designed and hooked by Kim Dubay, North Yarmouth, Maine, 1993.*

This makes an enclosed area to do your vertical hooking of the grass and creates a row at the edge. Hook two blades of grass at a time at varying heights. Start at the top and hook down, then turn your strip and hook in the opposite direction for the second blade of grass. This eliminates having a row of cut strips at the bottom of the rug.

Finally, fill in the background by following the contour of the design, and allow one or two rows to run along each edge of binding tape.

Sunflower Garden is available as a kit or as a printed pattern on burlap, monk's cloth, linen, or rug warp from Kim Dubay's company, Primitive Pastimes, 410 Walnut Hill Road, North Yarmouth, ME 04097, (207) 829-3725.

tical rows of hooking (see pattern in the "Exclusive Designs" section). The horizontal rails should be hooked side to side. Don't cut each strip at the end of the rails—instead, turn the strip and continue hooking in the opposite direction. This way you will avoid a noticeable line of cut ends at each side of the posts.

The sunflowers are next. Hook the centers in a gold-and-black herringbone—first outline them; then fill them in. Continue to hook the outside of the flowers with gold wool. (See the sidebar on page 55 for instructions on how to dye the gold using coffee instead of a commercial dye.) The flower stems are two rows hooked vertically, and the leaves are hooked in matching green wool.

For the grass, choose textured green wool that will show up against the green stems and leaves of the sunflowers—I used a tan-and-green herringbone. Another tip I give for hooking this grass is to hook between the fence posts in a U shape. Start on one side of a post, hook down and across the binding tape, and up along the side of the next post (see the pattern).

by Gail Dufresne

Sunflower Inch Mat

With a lesson on casserole dyeing

I designed my *Sunflower Inch Mat* with beginners in mind, so it has a little bit of everything in it, from a finely shaded flower with curving petals to a grid of straight lines. If getting just the right shading in the sunflower proves difficult, you can hook straight lines for a break (although for some, hooking straight lines is more of a challenge than curved ones). I also used a variety of materials, from recycled Pendleton shirts to textures to solid wools. Each is a little different from the other to work with and may take some getting used to. For example, when you are just learning to pull up loops, you may have a greater tendency to get your hook caught in loosely woven textures than in tightly woven solid wools.

Formulas and Casserole Dyeing

The dyes I used for this piece are PRO Chem brand dyes in the three primary colors: #119 yellow, #338 red, and #490 blue. I also used #672 black.

With just these four you can create any color you desire without using additional dyes, which is not only much more economical, but also the best way to really understand color.

All of these formulas are for use

> *"I designed my Sunflower Inch Mat with beginners in mind, so it has a little bit of everything in it, from a finely shaded flower with curving petals to a grid of straight lines."*

when dyeing 1/2 yard of wool (see the sidebar on page 62 for the quantity of wool needed for the inch mat). I used a speck of dye in two formulas, which I got by moistening a round toothpick and dipping it into the dry dye.

■ **The sunflower's center:** For my flower's center I used three textured wools, one of which was a perfect yellow-green, reminiscent of sunflower seeds, that I used as is. The orange texture is a tan herringbone spotted with 1/4 teaspoon of #119 yellow in 1

cup of boiling water and 1/4 teaspoon of #338 red in 1 cup of boiling water. The dark red texture is a pink tweed spotted with 1 teaspoon of #338 red and 1 teaspoon of #119 yellow.

■ **The petals:** Any nice yellow, gold, orange, or red swatch will work for the flower's petals, as sunflowers come in a range of colors. When choosing a swatch, keep in mind that the lightest values are used for highlights and the darkest for shadows. The overall flower color will be from the middle values of the swatch, so you will need more of those values. I dyed an 8-value swatch using 1/8 teaspoon of #119 yellow and 1/128 teaspoon of #338 red.

■ **Horizontal grid lines:** Spot natural

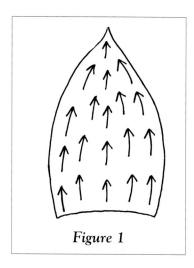

Figure 1

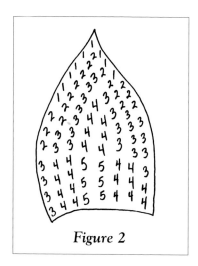

Figure 2

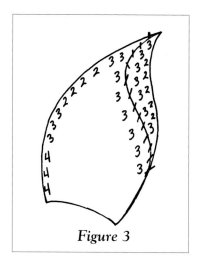

Figure 3

Sunflower Inch Mat, *17" x 17", #6-cut wool on rug warp. Designed by Gail Dufresne. Hooked by Mary Jean Whitelaw, Belle Mead, New Jersey, 2000.*

wool with a speck of #672 black for the lines.

■ **Lime-green squares:** Create a vivid green hue by spotting natural wool

with $1/2$ teaspoon of #119 yellow and $1/64$ teaspoon of #490 blue.

■ **Yellow squares:** Spot yellow wool with the swatch formula for these

squares.

■ **Red-grape squares:** Use pink wool for the red squares, and spot dye it with $3/4$ teaspoon of #338 red and $1/16$

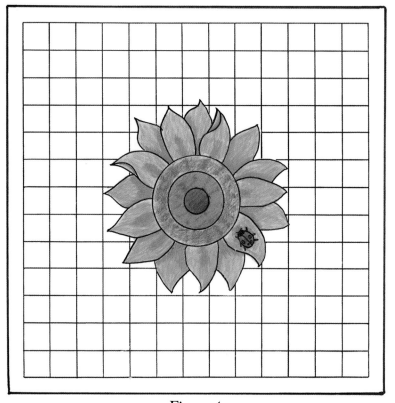

Figure 4

Transferring the Pattern to Backing

When selecting your backing, consider using cotton or linen rather than burlap. Cotton and linen last longer and are more evenly woven, which makes drawing grid lines much easier.

My pattern is 13 squares long and 13 wide, and each square is 1¹/4". The total pattern size is 17" x 17", including a ¹/2" border. Allow at least 6" on all sides of this pattern. Therefore, the backing should be at least 23" x 23".

Find the middle of your backing by folding it in half, and then fold it in half again the opposite way. Put a dot where the lines intersect; this is the center of your backing. Using a ruler, measure out ⁵/8" on either side of that middle dot, which will give you a 1¹/4"

teaspoon of #490 blue.

■ **Jade squares:** For these areas spot blue wool with ¹/2 teaspoon of #490 blue and ¹/4 teaspoon of #119 yellow.

■ **Vertical grid lines:** The vertical grid lines in this piece were hooked using some natural wool that was casserole dyed and some that was spot dyed. To dye using the casserole method, scrunch the wool into a casserole dish. Don't lay it flat—the hills and valleys of uneven color will give your rug more interest. This wool will be dyed with three different colors. First, mix ¹/8 teaspoon of #119 yellow in 1 cup of boiling water and pour the solution over ¹/3 of the wool in the pan. Next, mix ¹/8 teaspoon of #338 red and a speck of #672 black in 1 cup of water and pour this mixture over another third. Finally, mix ¹/16 teaspoon of

"When selecting your backing, consider using cotton or linen rather than burlap. Cotton and linen last longer and are more evenly woven, which makes drawing grid lines much easier."

#490 blue plus a speck of #672 black in water and pour this dye solution over the remaining third. You will need to add either citric acid or vinegar to set the dye. If you are using citric acid, sprinkle 1¹/2 teaspoons of it over the top of the wool. If you prefer to use the vinegar, pour ¹/3 cup of it evenly *around* the wool. Bake the wool for 1 hour at 300° F. For the dull yellow, spot dye natural wool with ¹/8 teaspoon of #119 yellow, ¹/64 teaspoon of #338 red, ¹/128 teaspoon of #490 blue, and ¹/128 teaspoon of #672 black.

square in the middle. Count the number of vertical threads in that square. Then use this thread count instead of a ruler to determine the size of each of the remaining squares.

Count to the correct number of threads; then with a soft leaded pencil (such as a carpenter's pencil), press down firmly between two vertical threads. Make sure the pencil point remains in that groove as you move the pencil slowly down the fabric. If the backing bunches up, ease the pressure on the pencil until

the backing flattens. Do not lift the pencil off the surface. Now do the same with the horizontal lines. When you come to the last line, measure out another 1/4" and add the border.

Transfer the sunflower motif to the rug using one of the methods mentioned on page 8. Make sure the center of the sunflower fits within the center square of the grid (the square that contains the center dot). Also see page 9 for finishing instructions. Believe it or not, you have to work on finishing your rug before you start hooking it.

Hooking the Sunflower

I recommend hooking the sunflower in either a #5 or #6 cut of wool.

When hooking any motif, hook just inside the printed line of the pattern, so the motif does not get too fat or distorted. Start by hooking the center of the flower, from the outside in, following the photograph to determine the placement of colors. Don't pack your loops, or your rug will bunch up.

Hook in the direction that the petal grows, from the center of the flower to the tip of the petal (see Figure 1 on page 58). Start with the petals that are on top; then move on to those where one side of the petal is underneath another. Finally, hook the petals that are underneath other petals. Save the first values of your swatch for the lighter, top petals and the last values for the darker, bottom petals. I used values 1 through 5 on the top petals and values 3 through 8 on the bottom ones. The petals should not be identical—they are not like that in nature.

To hook a realistic flower, mesh each value with the previous and subsequent values (Figure 2 on page 58). Do not skip values. Another way of determining the placement of values other than with a numbered sketch is by using a pencil drawing such as Figure 4 on page 60. You may find it easier to think about shades of color rather than numbers.

To make a point on the tip of a petal, hook up one side of the point and clip the strip at an angle, below the loops. This helps hide the cut. Then start down the other side of the point, beginning one stitch below where you cut the first side.

The flower in the pattern has two turned-over leaves. You can skip them if you want, but they are easy to do. Simply allow the lightest value to flow around the curved turn (Figure 3 on page 58).

You don't have to hook your bug in as much detail as the pattern shows. A round red blob with two black loops for a head and a few black spots will look just like a ladybug.

WOOL QUANTITIES

- **Sunflower petals:** One 8-value swatch, each value 3 1/2" x 12".
- **Sunflower center:** Small amounts of yellow-green tweed, orange textured wool (also used in squares), and dark red texture (also used in squares).
- **Ladybug:** Small piece of bright red and a bit of black.
- **Grid lines:** For the horizontal lines, 3/32 yard of dirty white. For the vertical, alternate 1/16 yard of casserole-dyed wool with 1/16 of spot-dyed dull yellow. I used three different colors for my grid lines, but you really need only one. You'll need 5/16 yard of wool for both the horizontal and vertical lines.
- **Blue squares:** 3/32 yard of blue plaid; I used recycled Pendleton shirts.
- **Lime-green squares:** 3/32 yard of lime-green.
- **Dark red squares:** 3/32 yard of dark red texture. This wool is also used in the sunflower's center.
- **Yellow squares:** 3/32 yard of spot-dyed yellow.
- **Red-grape squares:** 1/16 yard of spot-dyed red-grape.
- **Orange squares:** 1/16 of orange texture. This is also used in the sunflower's center.
- **Jade squares:** 1/32 yard of spot-dyed blue-green.
- **Border:** 1/8 yard of as-is blue plaid.

Hooking the Grids

After the sunflower is hooked, hook the grid lines. Hook them before the squares, as they will hold the squares in place. It does not matter whether the horizontal or vertical lines are hooked first, but be consistent. Normally, I would not recommend having strips crossing over each other

underneath the backing, as crossovers form bumps that will be the first spots of the rug to wear. If the inch mat is not going to be used on the floor, however, it is OK to have grid strips overlap, saving yourself many cut ends.

When hooking with the multicolored, casserole-dyed wool, pay attention to the way you hook the strips. For instance, if a strip you're hooking into the mat ends with a blue hue, hook the one next to it, starting with its blue end so that the blue runs into blue. This way there will be a seamless transition of color.

Hooking the Squares

You can hook the squares in a circular motion or in rows. To turn a corner without clipping your wool, simply turn the strip underneath in the direction you wish to hook, then proceed. Although not necessary, hooking adjacent squares in alternate directions—one horizontally, one vertically—reduces stress on the backing and adds interest to the design.

Return to the steaming and finishing instructions on page 9 to complete your mat. Then congratulate yourself on successfully learning a few lessons on dyeing and hooking and having such a nice mat to show for your efforts!

The Sunflower Inch Mat is available as a pattern or kit. It is also available as a larger pattern with three sunflowers. Write, call, or e-mail Gail Dufresne at 247 Goat Hill Road, Lambertville, New Jersey 08530, (609) 397-4885, gailduf @aol.com.

The following is a list of sources for the many patterns, projects, and products discussed in this book. Keep in mind that this is only a partial list of the many companies that sell these products. Most of these companies, and many more, advertise in *Rug Hooking* magazine. These companies can get you started with all the supplies you need to create hand-hooked rugs. The rest is up to you. Enjoy!

Rug Hooking Magazine
1300 Market Street, Suite 202
Lemoyne, PA 17043-1420
(800) 233–9055
www.rughookingonline.com
rughook@paonline.com
The indispensable source of rug hooking information and advertisers. Annual subscription for just $27.95.

Braid Aid Company
466 Washington Street
Pembroke, MA 02359
(781) 826–2560
Complete hooking and braiding supplies.

Country Colors
Maryanne Lincoln
10 Oak Point
Wrentham, MA 02093
(508) 384–8188
maryannelincoln@cs.com
Dye recipes and specialty dyed wool swatches.

Cox Enterprises
Verna Cox
10 Dube Road
Verona Island, ME 04416
(207) 469–6402
How-to videos and books on hooking and braiding for beginners and advanced crafters.

DiFranza Designs
25 Bow Street
North Reading, MA 01864
(978) 664–2034
www.difranzadesigns.com
Rug hooking patterns and supplies.

Dorr Mill Store
Rts. 11 and 103
Guild, NH 03754
(800) 846–3677
www.dorrmillstore.com
dorrmillstore@sugar-river.net
Quality wools, color palettes, patterns, kits, and much more.

Goat Hill Designs
Gail Dufresne
247 Goat Hill Road
Lambertville, New Jersey 08530
(609) 397–4885
gailduf@aol.com
Hooked rug patterns and supplies.

Mary Ann Goetz
10623 Cherrybrook Circle
Highlands Ranch, CO 80126
(330) 683–3330
Rug hooking patterns and kits.

Green Mountain Hooked Rugs
Stephanie Ashworth Krauss
146 Main Street
Montpelier, VT 05602
(802) 223–1333
vtpansy@together.net
Patterns, supplies, and the annual Green Mountain Rug School.

Harry M. Fraser Company
433 Duggins Road
Stoneville, NC 27048
(336) 573–9830
fraserrugs@aol.com
www.fraserrugs.com
Hooking cutters and complete rug hooking and braiding supplies.

Hooked Treasures
Cherylyn Brubaker
6 Iroquois Circle
Brunswick, ME 04011
(207) 729–1380
tcbru@suscom-maine.net
Rug hooking patterns and supplies.

House of Price, Inc.
177 Brickyard Road
Mars, PA 16046-3001
(877) RUG–HOOK
rughook@sgi.net
Fine quality hooking patterns, including Jane McGown Flynn designs.

Jacqueline Designs
Jacqueline Hansen
237 Pine Point Road
Scarborough, ME 04074
(207) 883–5403
www.rughookersnetwork.com
Over 400 primitive and traditional patterns.

Jane Olson Rug Studio
PO Box 351
Hawthorne, CA 90250
(310) 643–5902
www.janeolsonrugstudio.com
The total rug hooking and braiding
supplier for 27 years.

Mandy's Wool Shed
24 W. Wind Road
W. Gardiner, ME 04345
(207) 582–5059
Wide variety of excellent wools.

Miller Rug Hooking
Nancy Miller
2448 Brentwood Road
Sacramento, CA 95825
(916) 482–1234
millerrugs@aol.com
Hooking designs and kits.

Port Primitives
Barbara Brown
987 Back Road
Shapleigh, ME 04076
(207) 490–6933
Primitive patterns and supplies.

Primitive Pastimes
Kim Dubay
410 Walnut Hill Road
North Yarmouth, ME 04097
(207) 829–3725
Hooked rug kits, patterns, and
supplies.

Primitive Woolens
PO Box 251282
Plano, TX 75025-1282
Pat Brooks
(615) 230–5925
Jeanne Smith
(972) 542–4404
www.primitivewoolens.com
Hand-drawn primitive designs.

Pro Chemical & Dye
PO Box 14
Somerset, MA 02726
(888) 2–BUY–DYE
www.prochemical.com
Makers of PRO Chem dyes and
dyeing supplies.

W. Cushing & Company
PO Box 351
Kennebunkport, ME 04046
(800) 626–7847
www.wcushing.com
rughooks@wcushing.com
Dyeing supplies, hooks, patterns, kits,
and much more.

Woolley Fox, LLC
61 Lincoln Highway East
Ligonier, PA 15658
(724) 238–3004
www.woolleyfox.com
Primitive patterns, kits, and supplies.

Woolrich
Catalog Orders
Two Mill Street
Woolrich, PA 17779
(877) 512–7305
(Ask for operator 256)
rughooking@woolrich.com
Factory direct rug hooking wool.